THE
DEVIL IN THE
RED DRESS

PUBLISHED IN 2008 BY MAVERICK HOUSE PUBLISHERS.

Maverick House, Office 19, Dunboyne Business Park, Dunboyne,
Co. Meath, Ireland.
Maverick House Asia, Level 43, United Centre, 323 Silom Road,
Bangrak, Bangkok 10500, Thailand.

info@maverickhouse.com
http://www.maverickhouse.com

ISBN: 978-1-905379-59-0

5 4 3 2 1

The paper used in this book comes from wood pulp of managed forests.
For every tree felled, at least one tree is planted, thereby renewing natural
resources.

The moral rights of the author has been asserted.

Printed in Ireland by Colourbooks.

A CIP catalogue record for this book is available from the British Library.

To Michael,
With all my love, always.

The information contained in this book is based on evidence given in the trial of Sharon Collins and Essam Eid in the Central Criminal Court in 2008, and from publicly available court documents from the trial of Teresa Engle in California.

CONTENTS

ACKNOWLEDGEMENTS

My thanks to all the people who made this book possible particularly everyone at the Four Courts who made themselves available to check facts, dates, and spellings. Thank you to members of the Garda Síochana whose assistance in certain areas was an absolute lifeline and to those in County Clare who helped me find my way around the warren that is Ennis and pointed me in the right direction more than a few times.

Thanks especially to Diarmaid McDermott of Ireland International for his patience, and to everyone in the Four Courts media room during that trial. In particular thanks to Tom Tuite who convinced me to pitch this story, and Kathy Sheridan and Vivienne Traynor for all their encouragement. Thanks too go to Aoife Finneran of the *Evening Herald* and Sandra Murphy of the *Irish Daily Mail* for their help and answers to questions, and to Paddy and Brian of Courtpix and Garrett from Collins Photo Agency.

Also thank you to Jean Harrington at Maverick House for taking on the book and all her work getting it into shape.

To George Smith of www.globalsecurity.org and Commandant Peter Daly for their generous help on the thorny issue of ricin; also thanks to 'Mr Pink', the man behind www.hitman.us for getting in touch with me and allowing me to quote extensively from his website.

Special thanks go to Mal and Janina for reading early drafts and being calming influences and to Al, Emma, Wing, Natascha, Suzie, Rob and Ciarán for light relief and time out, not to mention patient answers to some of the technical questions.

Finally thank you to Michael, my husband, for having faith in me and always being there with a cup of tea and a hug.

CHAPTER 1:

THE QUEEN OF DIAMONDS

The way she told it, it was kismet.

'I remember noticing P.J. when I was a little girl, perhaps nine or ten. He was a grown man. I didn't know him until we started going out together but the memory of seeing him where he worked stayed in my mind. Then when I saw him walking into my shop eight and a half years ago, after seeing him out a few nights previously. I knew he was coming for me. It was almost like a premonition. It felt like I was expecting him even though I wasn't until he walked in.'

When P.J. Howard walked into Sharon Collins's shop, she believed he was going to change her life. The man she had noticed as a little girl, when he had only started to accumulate his wealth, was interested in her. His love promised access to the lifestyle she craved, not to mention security for her and her sons. She was determined to hook Howard for herself and luck was on her side. He was grieving, and she was available.

Collins painted it like a fairy tale, begging James Hamilton, the Director of Public Prosecutions, to drop the charges against her. She had met Howard in November 1998 and they had been together since she had moved into his house with her two sons for Christmas. But Collins, to all accounts, was more like the wicked stepmother than a defenceless ingénue, for she had been charged with plotting to kill the man who had made the fairy tale possible, and murder his two sons as well. Cinderella had become a femme fatale.

Over eight weeks in the summer of 2008, the convoluted tale of Sharon Collins and Essam Eid unfolded in front of a jury in Court Two at the Central Criminal Court in Dublin. As the trial wore on the number of people who came to catch a glimpse of the woman who became known as the 'devil in the red dress' grew steadily. They whispered at the back of the courtroom as they peered at the long wooden bench facing the jury box, where every day for 32 days the defendants took their seats.

'Isn't she a pretty little thing?'

'Is that the poker dealer?'

As the weeks went on and the salacious details emerged, their numbers grew. Many of them were the same people who came to watch every high profile murder trial. The anorak wearing pensioners, who always brought a plentiful supply of sweets, had their own seats staked out. They had turned up to watch the main event and, as the weeks wore on, they weren't disappointed.

Collins wasn't interested in them at all. Every morning she arrived in court dressed in a smart black trouser suit with a white top visible underneath, her blonde hair cut in business-like layers to just above the collar and her makeup understated, barely there. This was a different woman from the curvy pint-sized bombshell who turned up for her first court appearance in a short skirt and heels. She had lost a lot of weight since her arrest in February 2007; the angles in her face were now clearly visible, especially with the shorter hair. She now looked slightly harder, sharper; perhaps unsurprisingly as she was so close to losing everything she had spent so long building up.

Every morning her sons would wait for her in the lobby of the Four Courts where she would arrive after her daily consultation with her legal team. David, her youngest son, would arrive first. He would be joined by his older brother Gary, sombrely suited like his brother but looking more like his mother. When she joined them there was time for a few moments shielded from prying eyes in the partial shadow of a curved leather bench tucked beneath a stairwell. Sometimes they were joined by the boys' father, Noel Collins, who was a discreet presence throughout the trial to lend his support to his ex-wife and the two sons they shared. There were rarely other supporters though. She was involved in the kind of scandal that rarely touched the civilised middle class lives of her peers.

Just before 11a.m she would head into court to check that Essam Eid, her co-defendant who had offered himself as a hitman on the internet, had already taken his seat and every morning she would build a defensive fort of stationery in front of her. First would come the neat black folder that she came in clutching, which held the original statements from the day's witnesses. Then out came the pens, neatly placed within easy reach. Then the Polo mints and gum on which she and her sons constantly chewed as they listened to the evidence. On top of folder she would precisely place a large yellow Post-It pad. As the day progressed, she would write a steady stream of notes on the yellow pad, every now and then tearing off the top few pages to be folded over and given to David to pass on to her legal team. By the end of the day the back of the bench in front of her junior counsel would be feathered with over-lapping pages.

Collins never looked at her co-defendant during the trial but stared straight ahead at the jury when not writing, the calm and collected mask slipping every now and then to allow her expressive face to telegraph her reaction to each piece of evidence that stacked the prosecution case higher against her. Every so often, when the accusations got too close, she would lean towards one of her sons and whisper in a manner both intimate and urgent, staring earnestly into their eyes. When particularly damning evidence appeared she would lean towards them to share a private joke. But for the most part, despite the evidence against her, she gave the impression of attending the trial merely for politeness' sake, rarely showing any doubt in the security of her position.

At the far end of the bench her co-accused Eid joked with the prison guards. He had been in custody for almost two years, but he looked as if he was on holiday. Even in his never-varied casual outfit of black Nike jacket and jeans, he looked like a good fit for the role in which he was cast. His slightly receding hair was greying around the temples and his thick grey moustache had lost its battle to middle age. His sallow skin marked him out as an exotic character in the midst of the blue uniforms of the gardaí and prison warders, and the black gowns of the barristers. His appearance was so obviously not Irish that at the time of his arrest, gardaí had difficulty filling a line–up with a suitably cosmopolitan selection. If he felt pressured by his predicament he rarely showed it. He often chuckled to himself at the more bizarre pieces of evidence and smiled broadly as he watched the trial as if it was entertainment for him alone. He looked genuinely interested to see how things turned out.

The drama played out over eight weeks to the delight and fascination of the spectators, both media and general public. Collins fought her corner hard and refused to concede a single point to the prosecution. Every so often the tension would show in the courtroom by someone who would punctuate proceedings with much huffing and slapping of furniture.

The verdict finally came on 9 July 2008 on the 32nd day of the trial. After so many weeks of evidence it was perhaps not surprising that the jury took their time. They had asked frequent questions, asked to see numerous pieces of evidence and took multiple cigarette breaks when the tension got too much. In the end it took three days with two nights in a hotel. While the press settled in for the wait the tension was evident in both accused for the first time even though they both kept up a pretence at being relaxed. While Eid joked with the prison guards it was noticeable he was disappearing for more frequent cigarette breaks. By the second day he was spending most of his time in the cells that are hidden beneath the Four Courts, away from the curious eyes of press and public. Collins bobbed in and out of court like a restless bird, her supporters at her side. She spent most of the time sitting on the benches that are placed at regular intervals around the curved walls of the Round Hall or sitting under a stairwell. Everyone could see that her face was pale beneath her makeup and her eyes were hollowed by dark shadows. As the trial came to a close, she looked her age and the glamorous mask had finally slipped. As the hours slipped by, the tension slipped into tedium.

After lunch on the third day of deliberations, Justice Roderick Murphy asked the jury if they had reached a decision on any of the ten counts before them. It was a standard question that always prefaced the news that they no longer needed to reach a unanimous verdict. The jury looked surprised and the forewoman cleared her throat and nodded. They had come to an agreement on some of the counts. The tension in the courtroom suddenly ratcheted up drastically. A collective breath was held as the forewoman wrote the verdicts next to the box for each count on the issue paper they had been presented with when they retired. A pin dropping would have reverberated through the courtroom at that moment as the paper was passed to the registrar who looked at it briefly and turned to murmur something to the judge. The two accused sat impassively as the first verdicts were read out.

There was a baffled silence as the press and public tried to work out who had been convicted of what. The jury had returned verdicts on seven counts and as they were sent away to continue deliberating, the significance of what had happened spread around the court. The jury had decided unanimously that Sharon Collins had solicited a hitman to kill P.J. Howard and his two sons, although they still had to reach a decision whether it had actually been Eid with whom she had conspired; however, the jury had obviously been convinced of his intentions as a con man. He had been convicted of demanding €100,000 with menaces from Robert Howard when he had produced a stolen laptop but the jury had found him not guilty of other offences. As the jury left the room to decide whether Collins had been conspiring with Eid, everyone turned to see how the two accused were taking the news.

Collins had barely flinched as she was convicted time after time. She stared straight ahead at the jury as the registrar read out their decision. It was her sons who showed the shock and pain. Gary bowed his head as the first guilty verdict was read out, his head cradled in his hands hiding his face from the curious press. David stared at his mother, his face red as the tears streamed down.

The noise level in the court room rose again as journalists and barristers alike reached for their phones, and the public chattered amongst themselves about the implications of the piecemeal verdict. David stood up as if to move away from the burning scrutiny of the press less than two feet in front of him. Collins stood up as well and threw her arms around him, pulling his head down into her shoulder. Her former husband, Noel, appeared from the back of the court room and went to stand in front of the bench where Collins had been sitting, shielding her and his sons. Collins clung onto David, his shoulders shaking in her grip. It was only then that her own emotion showed and she buried her own face in her son's chest as the tears finally came. The enormity of her situation hit her fully for the first time and she suddenly looked like a lost little girl. The petite charmer had not managed to win over the crowd.

P.J. Howard had not been there to see the verdict, although his sons had appeared to watch the prosecution's closing argument. A statement emailed to the waiting press after the first verdicts were delivered asked for privacy. It was left to Collins's first husband to support his sons and ex-wife.

Noel led them out of the court and the waiting continued, but not for long. In under an hour at about 3 p.m. the jury came back with more verdicts. Sharon Collins had just been convicted of conspiring to kill P.J. Howard and his sons, Robert and Niall. As the last of the verdicts against her was read out Collins could be seen crying quietly. Gary and David, beside her as always, looked traumatised as they sat on each side of her, both of them gripping one of her hands.

The jury were still not finished, however, as they had not yet reached a verdict on whether Essam Eid was guilty on the three conspiracy to murder charges.

Eventually the judge called the jury back and asked them if they had reached a majority verdict on the conspiracy charges against Eid. He told the twelve worried and tired looking jurors that he was now giving them the choice of not returning a verdict. That if less than ten of them agreed they could agree to disagree and give up their deliberations. The forewoman looked at her colleagues who stared wearily back. It was now 5.30 p.m. and they had been deliberating for almost 11 hours. The forewoman told the judge they would need to discuss the matter in their room. Moments later they came back with news of a stalemate. Eid was neither guilty nor innocent of the conspiracy charge. There was a low babble in the courtroom as the assembled mass tried to work out the implications of this.

Collins's solicitor hurried over to her and they went into an urgent huddle. But ultimately she had been convicted and would be spending that night in jail. Her sons looked distraught as their mother was led away to the cells after Eid. The courtroom started emptying as the media machine geared itself up to start turning. For Sharon Collins, the fairy tale was definitely over.

CHAPTER 2:

IN SICKNESS AND IN WEALTH

Back in Ennis in County Clare the gossips really picked up speed, turning the story quickly from fairy tale to local legend. Rumours spread like mould in the damp humidity of the summer, the wettest for many years. But when the press descended they were met with polite smiles and stone walls. Ennis is too small a place to share gossip without having one eye open to see who's listening.

Prosperity may be apparent in the narrow twisting streets left over from a medieval history but the population is still only 18,000, many of them immigrants who have flocked to the town over the years. There are those who mutter darkly about the town becoming more cosmopolitan, who cling to the old Ireland where decades were needed before an interloper from the next parish became one of their own. But the story that hit the headlines did not concern any recent arrival. Both Sharon Collins and P.J. Howard were from local families and the story was embraced with a mixture of embarrassment and shock. Just as there were those who rubbed their hands over the juicy scandal that saw a local businessman and landlord embarrassed by a woman, there were others who shook their heads in wonder at a local girl from a good family wandering so far from what was right. For all its new found multiculturalism, not much has changed in Ennis over the boom years for those who have lived here all along. The big supermarkets only opened within the past few years and greengrocers still thrive among the old narrow streets. There is still a regular market, and the pubs sport wood panelling and old Guinness signs with floors of flag stones or red carpets. Today the town is beginning to feel the failing fortunes of a flagging economy, although the tourists still stream into the town. The maze of streets hide the numerous 'for sale' signs and there is consternation at several well-established businesses failing, but the boutique clothes shops remain. They cater for the 'ladies who lunch' and there are many lunching in Ennis. In fact the town prides itself on being the boutique capital of Ireland. Many shops house dresses that sell for hundreds of euros. These are not the shops that fear closure as the penny pinching begins; their patrons are women who don't need to worry about where the next pay cheque is coming from. Sharon Collins was once one of these women. As P.J. Howard's partner she enjoyed a powerful social standing that she enjoyed flaunting. There are many who have stories about her lady of the manor attitude.

She was born Sharon Coote, in the Hermitage area of Ennis in 1963, the youngest of three girls. Her family were not well off but were respectable and well-liked. Her mother and aunt had run a local cinema when she was a child and her uncle was the projectionist and sang in a local church.

As a family they kept themselves to themselves. Even as a girl, Collins did not move within a large group of friends, although this might have been a natural reaction to the situation at home. By the time she reached her teens her parents' marriage had floundered and her father moved out of the family home.

Sharon was the only Coote girl who stayed in Ennis. Her sisters also left Ennis to pursue their lives and careers. Sharon was a bright girl and could have gone far. She did her Leaving Certificate at a local school and won a place at the National Institution of Higher Education (which is now the University of Limerick) to do a course in computer studies. She enjoyed college. It was there she discovered that information had a nasty habit of lurking hidden in computer memory which could be unearthed by the authorities. She was even caught that way when a group of them played a prank and were discovered and punished. But this information, which could have been so useful to her, slipped her mind after she was overtaken by one of life's curve balls.

At 19 she dropped out of college to marry Noel Collins, her first husband, and later gave birth to her first son Gary. Collins discovered she loved being a mother and David was born two years later. She was devoted to her boys, but marriage was another thing entirely; neither of them had been ready to take that step and the strain began to show. In 1989 Noel moved out of the family home. Two years later they obtained a church annulment. As soon as the law changed in 1992 they divorced. Collins remained in the family home and they stayed friends for the sake of the children.

She would later say, 'I didn't have to resort to extreme measures at that time ... I can get on quite well with my ex-husband now. I think it's important for children that parents try to get along, even when the relationship breaks down. Otherwise, the children question their own worth.'

Collins was ruthless when it came to protecting her sons. She built up her own business, a kitchen design shop that sold bespoke kitchens and reclaimed antique fittings. With the property boom and home improvement fixation sweeping the nation it couldn't fail. She was standing on her own two feet for the first time in her life, in her own words she 'had come to the conclusion I didn't need a man.'

But despite her self sufficiency the single life was not for Collins so, in November 1998, when P.J. Howard walked into her life, she seized the chance.

P.J. Howard was seen as a particularly good catch. By the time he started going out with Collins he was a multimillionaire. He had built up his business from the car dealership he started in the seventies to a quartet of property companies that owned and managed an extensive portfolio of property across counties Clare, Limerick and Cork. An intensely private man, he was estimated to be worth €60 million, though Howard would describe himself as being merely 'comfortable'. He was certainly comfortable enough to sweep Collins off her feet and was in a position to shower her with expensive gifts. Within weeks she had moved into his large house on the Kildysart Road.

When they met, in November 1998, he was still in mourning for his partner of over six years, Bernie Lyons, who had died from cancer in the February of that year. He had met Bernie while he was still living with his wife, Theresa, who he had married in 1974. When the marriage broke down in 1992, he moved in with Bernie and they stayed together until her death. His two sons, Robert and Niall stayed with their mother. P.J. Howard and Bernie had been a very close couple and he was devastated when she died, but when he met Collins there was an immediate attraction.

He was captivated by her and he lost no time in showering her in expensive gifts; perfume, jewellery, a Rolex watch. The woman who had always fancied flash cars and the kind of security only money can buy allowed herself to be wooed. When he invited her and her sons to his house for Christmas she accepted and there they stayed, only leaving once after that for a couple of days the following February because Howard needed a few days to himself to mark the anniversary of Bernie's death. Collins may have been resentful of the position Bernie continued to inhabit in Howard's heart but she didn't show it.

According to all accounts Collins and P.J. Howard were madly in love at that time. It was still very early in the relationship when Howard asked her if she would be willing to spend the rest of her life with him. She agreed. They weren't able to marry since Howard had decided he did not want to divorce his estranged wife, but Collins accepted the situation for the time being. She had found the security she had been looking for. Despite their mutual need for one another they were hardly an obvious couple.

She was a flirtatious blonde 14 years his junior. There is no doubt that Collins was well aware of this disparity.

But it was one thing having her own opinion of how the relationship must look, other people thinking the same thing, however, was quite another. Collins was aware that some people might think she was simply a gold digger and she was determined that Howard would not come round to their way of thinking. She became the model partner. So much so that Howard would tell the court in her defence that she was selfless to a fault. If he ever gave her a few hundred euros to herself she would spend the money on her sons and only take a little perhaps for a new frock. Collins was building her persona well. In 2000 Howard underwent a quadruple bypass operation and Collins seized her chance to play Florence Nightingale. She tended his every whim, looked after his medication and nursed him back to full health. By the time he was back on his feet their relationship was stronger than ever.

Howard loved the sun and around the time he met Collins he had bought a penthouse apartment in the affluent Spanish town of Fuengirola in the Costa del Sol. The apartment was on the fourteenth floor of the Las Palmeras apartment and hotel complex. It was a stone's throw from the beach and packed with British and Irish bars and clubs. There was golf, a marina and the standard Malaga gift shop strip. There was even a Dunnes Stores if he should fancy a taste of home. As soon as the doctors gave him the all clear after his bypass operation he decided to pass over the management of his businesses to his sons and spend more time in Spain. He bought a boat, which, on the advice of a friend, he called 'the Heartbeat' in honour of his new lease of life. He moored it at the marina in nearby Benalmádena. Life was good and would have been perfect but for the fact that Collins's sons were still in school so she refused to spend as much time in Spain as he wanted her to. It was one of the few things they rowed about but until the boys had left school there wasn't much to be done.

Then in 2003 a tragedy hit the family that would change everything. 20-year-old Niall Howard arrived home for lunch one day to the house he shared with his mother Theresa. She was not downstairs as normal so he went to find her. He found her in bed. She had suffered a severe brain haemorrhage and was dying. Niall was traumatised and the tragic event impacted on the whole family. Niall moved into Ballybeg House, unable to continue living in the place where his mother had died. Collins is said to have treated him as one of her own children and they became very close over the next few months. Niall didn't want to stay in Ballybeg House though. After a month he moved into a self-contained flat in the house his brother had bought in Doora on the outskirts of Ennis.

He decided to raze his mother's house and completely rebuild it. Knowing Collins had experience in interior design he asked for her help. Collins gave it gladly. She had become a vital part of the Howard family, and was even helping out in the family business. Several days a week she would sit at reception taking care of general secretarial duties. It stopped her from being a kept woman, although Howard still topped up her €850 a month wages. She would protest she wasn't a very good secretary but she had already impressed P.J. Howard with her computer skills, which had developed and updated considerably since her abandoned course in Limerick all those years ago. All in all they were a solid family unit.

However, Theresa's death opened up another possibility. For the first time in the relationship marriage was on the table—as far as Collins was concerned. She made it clear that she had always wanted to marry again. There was nothing to stop them now. Howard was more reticent but he wanted to make her happy—so he proposed. She was ecstatic. They planned a quiet wedding in Rome in October 2005 with a lavish reception for all their friends and family in Spanish Point, County Clare when they got back.

But there was still a hitch. Howard was aware how much work both Robert and Niall had put into the family businesses since they had been old enough to start working in them. Since his bypass they were running the family empire between them. They were both directors and Robert now handled the day to day running of Downes & Howard, the flagship business of the family's portfolio. Howard wanted to make sure they were rewarded for all their hard work. As far as he was concerned, they had to inherit the business after his death. That was where the problem lay. A wedding would put Collins into the front running in the inheritance stakes, so a solution had to be found. Collins for her part was absolutely determined to get married. She put her foot down and offered him an ultimatum. If she didn't get a wedding ring he wouldn't get her. Howard looked desperately around for a solution. He didn't want to hurt anyone. His sons were important to him and he was aware how hard they had worked, but Collins was the woman he loved and he was not about to let her walk away.

Then he thought of it. A prenuptial agreement could solve all their problems. Howard and Collins both contacted their solicitors to draw up the documentation but it wasn't going to be that easy. Howard discovered that a prenuptial agreement wasn't worth the paper it was written on under Irish law. No matter what they signed and how they wanted Howard's assets divided up, Collins would still end up floating to the top of the pile when it came to heirs.

In the end they agreed to compromise and decided to make private vows to each other in a church, but the first cracks in the relationship began to show. It was all the more difficult to look past the more fundamental problems that had been running in the background throughout the relationship. Collins began to feel the strain. She wanted the security of a marriage, as she knew she had no legal rights to his fortune should their relationship break up, or should anything happen to him. She felt that she had put in the work, and she deserved her share of his wealth.

She knew that she would have to be patient to get what she wanted, and so she bided her time and went ahead with the private exchange of vows in November 2005. It wasn't ideal, though, and she secretly began to fume about the situation she found herself in. She pretended that she was perfectly content with the status quo, but in truth it began to play on her mind until she was consumed by what she saw as a problem. She wanted to get married.

If Howard wouldn't marry her, she would find her own way around the problem. After all, she had looked after herself in the past and she could do it again; but this time she decided to take drastic measures.

With this level of bitterness bubbling away inside her, for Collins the fairy tale had turned into a ticking bomb. On 2 August 2006, sitting at her computer in Downes & Howard, she would take the step that would ruin her life and wreck the lives of those around her. After a little desultory surfing Collins typed in the address of the Yahoo home page and applied to open an email account with the web based service that she assumed could offer her total anonymity for what she planned to do next.

She had a plan; she just needed an anonymous email account to put it into action. As she sat and thought about her situation, suddenly the words of an Eagles song, Lying Eyes, floated into her head. Her own situation could easily be said to bear a striking resemblance to it.

'A rich old man
And she won't have to worry
She'll dress up all in lace and go in style …
You can't hide your lying eyes,
And your smile is a thin disguise.'

She thought she had created a 'perfect' email address with the alias 'Lying Eyes'. To complete the email, she simply added the year in which she had become P.J. Howard's partner—lyingeyes98@yahoo.ie.

In the course of her trial it would become a byword for the more bizarre aspects of the case but for the moment it was something only slightly more than a private joke. Spurred on by her new-found anonymity she started searching for a final solution. The answer she hit upon would set into motion a plot that would span both sides of the Atlantic Ocean. For the object of her ardour and ambition, sitting alone on his yacht in the Costa del Sol, there would be no happily ever after.

CHAPTER 3:

GAMES AND DAMES

While Collins was becoming increasingly dissatisfied with her lot, the enterprise that would prove her undoing was being born. Perhaps if she had known how hitmanforhire. net came into being, or who was behind the website she would have thought twice about registering. The smiling joker driving the yellow Corvette was not the dapper Sicilian hitman the website had promised, but a 49-year-old Egyptian poker dealer in Las Vegas, whose love life was every bit as complex as the one she had complained of herself.

Essam Ahmed Eid was born in Cairo in 1955, the year before the Suez Crisis brought economic and social upheaval. The world that Eid was growing up in was changing rapidly. The new Egyptian government had set about removing the signs of British occupation and a new cultural nationalism was in the air. It was a turbulent place to grow up. Eid was conscripted into the Egyptian army as a young man. He would later tell gardaí that he had once been a warrior and knew how to kill with his bare hands. But a career in the military did not suit the young Eid and he earned himself a degree in accountancy before leaving for America and the promise of a new life.

Eid was a charmer. Anyone who watched his trial could see how the boy from Cairo had grown into a charming man, ready with a smile or a joke for anyone. He turned up at the Four Courts each day in the white and blue prison services van that brought the most hardened criminals in to face the courts. The poker dealer had been refused bail as he was considered too big a flight risk. Every morning he walked the gamut of photographers standing outside the side gate to the Four Courts, a more practical entrance for those in custody than the fortress-like main gate. He treated the snappers with nonchalant disregard, laughing as he shared a joke with his prison guard escort. He would often be smiling in his daily photograph, unusual for someone in his position. He even charmed his cell mates in Limerick Prison, becoming the chief lecturer in a series of impromptu poker classes where he could give them the benefit of his gambling expertise.

He would joke that he wanted Al Pacino to play him in the movie of the trial, but the character that was painted by his defence was more bumbling Cohen Brothers villain than Noir gangster. The plot that had led him to the Irish courts could have been brilliant in its execution if greed had not got in the way.

He might have seemed a convincing gangster when he arrived on an Irish doorstep on an autumn evening, but Eid's involvement in organised crime had only lasted for two outings, both of which ended in arrest. Essam Eid was no career criminal. As a friend of his told the FBI, he liked to 'talk the talk not walk the walk.' If he had continued talking he might have still had a job in the glamorous world of Vegas nightlife rather than earning his criminal record in an Irish jail.

He tried his hand at various careers including accountancy, and also worked as a travel agent before moving to Las Vegas where he discovered his talent for poker dealing. He lived and worked in a world where the names of Bugsy Siegel and Lucky Luciano were still legend, providing his choice of alter ego. Vegas, with its associations with Sinatra and the Rat Pack, the mob and prohibition, was the perfect place for hitmanforhire.net to be spawned. When Eid applied to work at the upmarket Bellagio casino he didn't have a stain on his character. He was deemed a suitably steadfast employee to oversee the poker games that saw thousands of dollars change hands.

The Bellagio prides itself on being a little bit classier than some of the other casinos on the strip, and is situated next door to Sinatra's old stomping ground, Cesar's Palace, and the location for Ocean's 11. Every evening the massive fountains at the front of the Bellagio give balletic displays to a soundtrack of classical music and movie themes. The shops in the adjoining arcade sell a pricier kind of tat with designer labels and the Fine Art Gallery and conservatory boast a hot house 'botanical garden' albeit with giant plaster frogs and over sized silk poppies. It's the archetypal image of a Las Vegas casino, all bright lights and shiny things; gold glinting on the edge of every glance, the carpet muffling the footsteps of the tourists, the gamblers and the desperate.

Eid worked as a dealer on one of the forty or so poker tables, open for business day and night. During work he kept a very low profile dealing the cards and making sure all was fair as the stacks of chips rose and fell. All that money with the power that went with it must have been tempting. After all, his job at the Bellagio paid only $6.50 an hour; a sum barely above minimum wage, although it wasn't the take-home pay that made working in a casino worthwhile—it was the tips. He could make hundreds in tips in one night. Eid would later tell gardaí he could earn up to $100,000 dollars a year, mainly from tips from the five star punters. In the world of high stakes poker, people show their gratitude to the person who dealt them the winning hand. It costs nothing to flip a chip from the growing pile in front of you to the dealer, especially when it keeps a losing run at bay. But while the money was good, Eid had a problem keeping it. Despite spending his working day watching the losers as well as the winners, he fancied his chances at making it big. The problem was that luck frequently deserted him when he finished work for the night and went to the Cannery Casino in North Las Vegas.

The Cannery was a far cry from the Bellagio. In the smoke-filled casino with a 1940s theme, metal legged chairs crowd around green baize gaming tables where Eid wasn't the only one losing money. His money just seemed to evaporate and the idea of a scheme that would provide a steady flow of cash, or better still, a generous tax free cash injection seemed ever more attractive. For Eid was a man with responsibilities. He had a house, a child and a wife to care for and another wife had just moved in. A conscientious Sunni Muslim, he had grown up with the belief that polygamy was not just the preferable but the honourable thing to do. The Nevada authorities refused to accept polygamous unions but Eid did not believe in monogamy and, after a string of girlfriends, he chose a second wife, Teresa Engle. As his finances started to dwindle he started looking for alternatives—and found them in a website called hitmanforhire.net.

Eid's domestic arrangements were subject to endless speculation over the long weeks of his trial but the story behind them might have been far more mundane than they appeared. His original wife, Lisa Marsee, seems to have been totally unaware that a second marriage may or may not have taken place. She declined to be interviewed for this book but her story has already been told in the American courts. Eid met Lisa Marsee in Michigan during the Spring of 1999.

He had been under pressure from his friends to settle down and provide a stable home and mother figure for his young daughter, Aya, who was a child from a previous relationship. Lisa was a naïve, trusting woman who, at 33, wanted to start a family. She saw the chance to step into a ready-made family and took it. Eid was working at a travel agents at the time, as a wholesale sales rep for Suisse Air Airlines. He certainly seemed like a dependable type of guy. They were married within the year. But appearances can be deceiving. Eid did not turn out to be the model husband she was hoping for. According to friends who were around at the time, Eid was a serial philanderer who would have a different girlfriend every other month. Lisa either didn't know or turned a blind eye. It wasn't a perfect situation but she didn't want to leave him; he could be so charming when he wanted to be. Friends had speculated that Eid could be quite manipulative with the woman in his life. He was a very strict father and liked to be the man of the house. Lisa certainly never stood up to him over his repeated affairs. But then, none of them lasted very long, that is until he changed jobs and started working as a dealer in a casino in Detroit in 2003, where he met Engle.

She was living in Detroit with her husband Todd and her young daughter. She was a frequent weekend visitor to the casino where Eid was a dealer. She sat at the Egyptian's table to play her poker and the two quickly struck up a friendship. Eid gave her the full benefit of his charm and Engle was very conscious that he 'really wanted me'. They would talk for hours, sharing experiences and laughing at each others' jokes. The flirting developed into an affair. Eid spun her the old line that his marriage was over and he was heading for divorce. Engle was bored with her married life and wanted a change. So a passionate relationship developed that would lead them both into taking ever more ludicrous risks until they both ended up in jail. It was a union of two people who appealed to the other's worst character traits. Ashraf Ghardbeiah, an old friend of Eid's thought Engle was a bad influence. The Saudi Arabian had worked with Eid ten years previously in the Cosmopolitan Travel Store. He was pleased to meet someone from a similar background and when they discovered they both had daughters of a similar age their friendship flourished. Ghardbeiah knew that Eid was something of a womaniser. He didn't approve; his own marriage had hit the rocks after his wife cheated on him, but Eid told him to mind his own business, and he did so out of respect for his friend. But when Eid met Engle he began to worry about his friend. He suddenly bought himself a bright yellow Corvette and stopped going fishing or hanging out with his friends. Ghardbeiah was convinced that Engle was the driving force behind this new found recklessness. He had first met her when Eid had rang him looking for a loan sometime in 2003. He agreed to lend the money and Eid had turned up at his office with the tall, brown haired woman he soon knew as Teresa. At first he wasn't too concerned. He assumed she was just another of his friend's many girlfriends. But slowly Eid began to change. Then something happened that really worried him. Sometime around late 2005 when Ghardbeiah was working as a reserve police office, he received a call from Eid who told him that he had needed a friend with a gun. Eid was matter of fact about the favour he needed. He wanted someone to dispose of Engle's husband.

Ghardbeiah was shocked, he was sure that his friend was not a violent or threatening kind of person at all. He immediately called a police friend of his who advised him to play along until he had enough evidence to press charges. Ghardbeiah was worried that if he didn't agree to the idea his friend might be crazy enough about this woman to find someone else to do the job. But when he rang Eid back a couple of days later, Eid was offhand. Engle had changed her mind he said.

'Sorry for putting you to all the trouble. It's fine now.' Ghardbeiah thought that was the end of the matter, but it would be a few more months before he would find himself in Ireland meeting with Engle and talking about killing two men neither of them had ever met.

So who was this woman who had gotten Eid to take leave of his senses? It very much depends who you talk to. The woman who appeared in court in Dublin and was later sentenced to eight months in an American prison for her part in one of the scams arising out of hitmanforhire.net was tall and rather gangly with tightly curled, brown frizzy hair. Her voice was either a mousy whisper that hardly managed to limp out of the witness box into the court room or a rasping smoker's voice that hinted at a coarse personality and a foul tongue. She was either a victim going along with the brutal orders of her oppressor out of a passivity born of Stockholm Syndrome or the main architect of a murderous plot.

Engle was born in Kentucky to Janice and Jimmy Brock. She was the couple's first child and her mother almost died having her—she would later claim that her parents had it in for her from the start. According to Engle, her father never forgave her for almost killing her mother while he was away in another State working to support his new family. Her mother exacted an almost daily revenge with regular beatings with a fresh switch cut from the tree outside the family home. Engle claimed that out of four children, she had the worst childhood. Her brother Mike was born a year after her, a sister, Dawn three years later and lastly, the baby of the family, Brandy. When Engle was three or four the family moved to Ohio, where they remained. Engle described herself as 'a bad child, a mean girl.' Her Aunt Joyce who had looked after her as a baby while her mother recovered from the difficult birth claimed that Engle's father told the family he 'never loved a child until Dawn was born. She was the golden girl, Brandy was the baby, Mike was the reject and Teresa was the black sheep.' Mike had contracted polio at the age of four or five and was confined to a wheelchair. His disability and the fact he suffered from severe Obsessive Compulsive Disorder meant that he would never be able to move out of the family home or have a normal life. Engle would tell a psychologist that apart from her Aunt Joyce, the only family member who had ever shown her any kind of love was her maternal grandmother. She had shared a bed with her grandmother until she was five years old and was close to her until she died.

Engle found herself pregnant before she was out of her teens but she didn't keep the baby or marry the father. She met Todd Engle soon after this, when she was 19. Todd was twelve years older and offered the possibility of the stability and affection she was looking for. They had a whirlwind romance and married after only a month. Engle was desperate for a normal family and wanted to have a child. Unfortunately Todd had neglected to tell her before they got married that he had had a vasectomy and their attempts to reverse the procedure were unsuccessful. So in 1989 Engle divorced Todd for the first time. Her biological clock was ticking by this stage so she found herself a younger man, James Connors, who she knew as Jim. Connors was 'nice' but was unfortunately a drug addict. Even so, in 1991, they got married and in 1993 Engle gave birth to their daughter Cheyenne. Despite Engle's best efforts Connors's addiction made happy families impossible despite his repeated spells in Rehab. He was spending frequent spells in jail and by 2000 Engle had finally had enough. She took Cheyenne and moved out. The house was lost when Connors was unable to meet the mortgage payments. The debts mounted uncontrollably and they ended up having to file for bankruptcy. Engle moved back home with Cheyenne and filed for divorce. Around this time her beloved grandmother died. The news sent Engle into a downward spiral and she was hospitalised for a major depressive episode, the second in her adult life. When she got out of hospital Todd was waiting for her. They started dating again and Engle moved in with her sister Dawn who was also raising a young daughter. But more change soon followed when Dawn announced she was moving to another town. Engle jumped to the safest ship. Todd had moved to Michigan and wanted another shot at marriage. Everything was looking rosy and it finally looked as if she would get the 'normal family' she had always longed for.

But it turned out Engle didn't suit normality as much as she might have hoped. By 2003 she was going to play poker every Friday night at a local casino. She always sat at the table with the warmest welcome, the table run by Essam Eid. But even this didn't run smoothly. Engle might have jumped between men but she liked them to give her their undivided attention and she had soon discovered that Eid was already married. After about five months of being the other woman Engle upped sticks again and moved back to Ohio with Cheyenne, walking out on both her husband and her lover. She was no match for Eid's silver tongue and views on polygamy and his persistence eventually paid off. Engle was now spending her time travelling between Ohio and Michigan. When Eid decided to try to break into the Las Vegas scene in November 2004 she followed him but, soon got cold feet when she discovered he hadn't divorced Lisa and moved straight back to Ohio. After more perseverance from Eid, she was back in Vegas, having left her daughter with her sister. She and Eid set up their love nest at 4467 El Quinta, Las Vegas, the address that hitmanforhire.net would be registered from in April 2005, and for several months things seemed to be going well. Engle had a job in the accounts department of the Hotel Riviera and Eid had started working in the Bellagio. They even got married, despite the fact neither of them had divorced the people they were already married to.

But the idyll wouldn't last; Lisa was never far away. She too had followed Eid to Vegas. She and Aya moved there in July 2005 and Eid bought a house for them at 6108 Camden Cove Street, a residential area in North Las Vegas. This was desert suburbia where identical white bungalows sheltered from the sun under red tiled roofs. In the front, where in a more temperate climate would grow shrubs and picket fences, were patches of parched grass. When Engle found out Lisa was still on the scene she once again returned to Ohio, but she was back in Vegas by October or November 2005. Lisa recalled meeting her at one of the local casinos.

Eid told Lisa that Engle was an old friend from Michigan and she thought no more about it. From then on Engle was a regular visitor to 6108 Camden Cove Street. She was there for the Thanksgiving dinners at the house and she and Lisa would often bump into each other at social gatherings involving the old gang from Michigan.

Lisa was having difficulty finding work in Vegas. She had worked in telecoms in Michigan and the set up was different in Nevada so her skills were redundant. After trying unsuccessfully to find a job doing something she was vaguely qualified to do, Lisa decided that the only option was to retrain. She started a course in massage therapy and got immersed in her studies. When, sometime around June 2006 Eid told her that his friend Engle had lost her job and was having difficulty meeting the rent she reluctantly agreed for Engle to move in until she was back on her feet. She thought the arrangement was only for a couple of days but Eid and Engle had other plans.

In some ways it turned out to be quite useful having Engle around. Aya was a headstrong teenager and clashed frequently with her father over her choice of boyfriends. Engle was able to act as a go between, and she and Aya became quite close. Aya knew that Engle had feelings for her father and had a sneaking suspicion that her father felt the same. Ashraf Gharbeiah visited his friend around this time and noted what an awkward situation the whole thing was. It seems that only Eid was happy with the situation. He had even managed to persuade Lisa and Engle to take part in threesomes with him. Engle was far more experimental in bed than Lisa was; she even enjoyed the rough sex he was so fond of.

Lisa was reaching a crucial point in her studies and needed peace and quiet at home. Eid and Engle were more than happy to go out to the Cannery in the evenings to give her time to study. She didn't have time to raise the subject of Engle's continued residence in the house until after she had finished her exams.

Engle tells a completely different story of her time in 6108 Camden Cove Street. She was later arrested in California for attempting to extort money and told a psychologist, as part of her defence, that she had soon become afraid of and intimidated by Eid. She painted a picture of sexual slavery and virtual imprisonment. Eid made her sell her car, she said, and would make her come to work with him in the casino so he could keep an eye on her.

It's a startlingly different picture to the one described by both Aya and Lisa who said that Engle quickly got a job after she moved in, doing accountancy for a construction business. She had her own car and came and went as she pleased. Lisa said the only time she had ever heard Eid shout at Engle was when she hadn't said something to Aya he had wanted her to.

Engle, however, paints a picture of horrendous abuse. She claims that the rough sex was nightly and not content with wrestling between the sheets, Eid would also slap her around in front of Lisa. He would slap her if she made a mistake, again if she cried. He made her cut off all contact with her family.

'I was a complete nervous wreck. I could not eat or sleep. I was terrified all the time.'

She claimed that Eid showed distinctly psychopathic tendencies.

'He made me massage him all the time. I wasn't allowed to stop.'

She went on, 'He made me eat his shit, all of his bodily fluids. I had to drink his urine and mucous. Even blood. Scabs. Every night I would say to myself, "Please God don't let me live through this night".'

She told the psychologist she had gone through her ordeal as if it was an out of body experience.

'I knew it wasn't me, doing these things. I watched myself do all this shit he made me do. I was not me. I was like that TV show Bewitched; I was dissociated. Out of my body watching myself.'

She said she was relieved 'to the point of collapse' when she was arrested in Ireland because she could finally get away from Eid.

Her description of this alleged abuse was vivid enough to convince gardaí although not quite so readily accepted by the FBI and the prosecution in the Royston[1] trial. The Bureau pointed out that she had been to Ireland on an earlier occasion and could have easily called the gardaí at this stage. They viewed her stories as self serving and pointed out that they were completely unsubstantiated. Neither Lisa nor Aya saw any of the abuse she mentioned and both said that Engle had plenty of privacy at 6108 Camden Cove. Certainly emails sent from Engle's account to Eid's yahoo account after their arrests in Ireland, did not suggest a battered spouse.

'I dreamt about you last night. I can't seem to get you off my mind.'

Aya maintained that, rather than being coerced into acting illegally, Engle was besotted with her father and took her actions out of love rather than any other reason. Eid would later insist that he had been set up by the women in his life. He said that his hours in the casino would have made it impossible to conduct a flirtatious relationship with Sharon Collins, besides, he already had two wives! Whatever the dynamics of their relationship, Eid and Engle were quite a pair. Their scheme to fund the gambling that they both so enjoyed would land them both in jail. What may have seemed like the perfect way to get rich quick ended up losing them the pot.

---

1 Engle and Eid attempted to extort money from a girl call Lauryn Royston and her boyfriend after his former girlfriend contacted hitmanforhire.net. Royston contacted the police and Engle was arrested.

CHAPTER 4:

QUEEN OF HEARTS

Despite what would be insinuated during her trial, Collins was very much a one man woman and the man she was determined to get was P.J. Howard. She had been a loyal partner and by 2005 she felt she had paid her dues. She had been his rock, and nursed him through his bypass operation. She had treated his two sons as her own and she wanted some recognition of her position within the family. She wanted to get married. She had never made a secret of the fact that one day she would like to marry again and as far as she was concerned, that day had come.

She started dropping hints in the way a charming woman can. Their relationship may have had its bumpy patches but it was still as strong as ever. She started planning a big society wedding in Dromoland Castle Hotel. She'd fallen in love with the place after they'd had a party for her 40th birthday there. She had even got as far as inviting friends … until Howard came back with the bombshell. He wanted a prenuptial.

But even after she learnt that Howard would never marry her without a prenuptial agreement she kept pushing him. When her charm didn't work she started issuing an ultimatum and insisted that a solution be found. Howard did his best. Whatever faults she found with him he was undeniably smitten with her and would do whatever it took to make her happy, as long as that didn't mean his sons would be left without.

Collins was insistent. Why couldn't they carry out their plan to get married in Rome? If Howard didn't find a solution she would walk out, even if it did mean starting again. Howard didn't want to lose her so a compromise was suggested. Why didn't they take the trip to Italy anyway? They might not be able to get married but he didn't want any other woman. The two appeared to be genuinely in love. There was nothing stopping them pledging themselves to each other in some other way. Collins wasn't keen but as she realised there was no other way, she slowly agreed. During the trip they would go to a little church somewhere and take their own vows. It wouldn't matter if there was no priest involved; all that mattered was that God was watching and knew how much they were in love. Collins allowed herself to be talked around. It wasn't perfect but it was the best she was going to get.

It wouldn't work if no one knew what they'd done though. They couldn't invite friends to a private church pledge without a priest. No one would understand so Howard suggested yet another compromise. The trip to Italy was to take place in November. Why not kill two birds with one stone and turn the Downes & Howard Christmas party into a wedding reception. They could send out invitations and it would be just like the real thing. Collins agreed and had invitations printed on cream card with embossed writing and gold rings on the front. If they were going to share the Downes & Howard Christmas party she was going to leave no one in any doubt that this was her night. If Collins had her way, the mere lack of a priest wouldn't stop her from becoming Mrs P.J. Howard. She threw herself into the plans with gusto. Collins was determined to keep up the façade all the way through. There would be a photographer and a new dress. She planned things as thoroughly as she would have planned her real wedding. Perhaps P.J. Howard was struck by the degree of her planning, or maybe the invitations seemed just a little bit over the top. He wanted to make absolutely sure he didn't accidentally end up married for real. Collins was keen to put his mind at rest. It wouldn't do to have him back out of her matrimonial extravaganza at this point. She typed up a short document to pacify him. They both signed their names to the fact that they had no intention of getting married on their trip to Italy and were not now, or ever would be, married to one another. The document was dated and they both kept a copy to give to their solicitors just so there could be no confusion in the future.

P.J. Howard delivered his copy straight away. Collins was a little slower. In the end she only delivered the single sheet of A4 paper when her motives had come under suspicion and the gardaí had already shown an interest in her. Suddenly the lines drawn up in the offices of Downes & Howard seemed an important alibi so she lodged them with her solicitor. Better late than never!

In November 2005, however, she was content to pretend that the letter and Howard's stubbornness were just a bad dream that couldn't get in the way of the Italian fairy tale she was intent on enacting. Collins planned the day with great care. After all, it was the only time Howard was actually going to pledge his love for her in a church, despite the lack of priest and witnesses. They decided that a little church in Sorrento would be perfect for their vows, choosing a romantic venue for their special day. They dressed up and Collins even found a local photographer, so that it could never be denied. Then one afternoon they went to their church and stood in front of the altar. On their own out of the Italian sun they said a couple of prayers and then pledged their undying love to the cool shadows in the corners of the empty pews.

Then it was over. Collins would have to wait until she was back in Ireland to hear the applause and congratulations from her friends and family. But at least she could start calling herself Sharon Howard. As far as P.J. Howard was concerned, everything was sorted now. His assets were safe, the document ensuring they were safe was with his solicitor and he had met the woman he loved more than half way. The rest of the holiday was the start of their honeymoon. As they posed for photographs, it seemed like the perfect day and the best possible way to mark the love they shared.

When the holiday was over and they had returned to Ireland, Collins started telling her friends they had really got married that day in the little church. Howard wasn't worried. He knew that there was a document saying otherwise in a safe place in his solicitor's office. So he didn't mind that most of the guests who attended their 'reception' party in the four star Admiralty Lodge Hotel thought a wedding had taken place. He knew it was all make believe. It didn't bother him that the staff at the hotel thought they were catering for a wedding party, or that the large white cake had a little bride and groom on it, or that the invitations had a distinctly matrimonial feel to them. It all made Collins happy after all.

The people who mattered the most to him knew the truth. Howard had sat down his elder son Robert and explained the whole situation to him. It was unfortunate that the boys weren't as enthusiastic about it as the happy couple but he was a responsible father and had made sure everything would be kept safe for them. He just wanted to make his Sharon happy.

All in all it was a successful night. The forty or so guests lifted a glass of champagne to the happy couple and when they cut the cake there were few who had any idea it had not been baked to mark recent nuptials. Robert and Niall Howard were there with their girlfriends and Gary and David were there for their mum as well. It was a perfect family occasion and carried on long into the winter night. Collins kept the photographs from the festive celebrations on her computer and would later provide proof of the smiles on the faces of Robert and Niall as identifying features for her internet hitman.

But ultimately it just wasn't enough. Collins was secretly far from satisfied. Even as she played the newly wed she was exploring ways to shore up her position. If Howard wouldn't take her to a church to make his vows before a priest then she would just have to find a way to do so without him. It just wasn't the same calling herself Sharon Howard without the documents to back it up. So without her partner's knowledge she went on the internet and by the time they were celebrating their supposed nuptials with family and friends she was already well on the way to becoming Mrs Sharon Howard for real … on paper at least.

It hadn't taken long to find the first mention of proxy marriages. It appeared that they had done it wrong in Italy. They'd had no priest and therefore no marriage whereas, according to some of the sites she was now reading, they could have stayed at home, filled out a few forms and magically, they would be man and wife without any fuss, and a reluctant groom mightn't even have to know. Collins started her research and eventually found somewhere that looked like it might do the job. The problem was that a simple single proxy marriage wasn't good enough. A proxy marriage is the kind of marriage where the other spouse is unable to come to the wedding in person. If you want to marry someone on death row this would be a way around the prison authorities not issuing a day pass. In this situation the proxy attends the wedding in place of the jailbird and the marriage legally stands—once it's been consummated. This kind of marriage has been around for years and has allowed soldiers on active duty to marry their sweethearts back home. It has even allowed a cosmonaut on the International Space station to get married to a girl back home. They were common in past centuries among nobility and royalty when one of the parties was too young, too old or too mad to be brought out in public. A proxy marriage was the perfect solution when one party didn't even know about the pressing need to get married.

But Collins had an added complication. She had signed a piece of paper with Howard promising him they would not get married. She knew he would not agree to any marriage, even a proxy one. It rather defeated the purpose of vowing not to get married. If Collins were to suddenly go to Mexico, Howard would either want to come, or want to know what she was doing there. She just wouldn't be able to get away with it. So a double proxy was the only way forward. This made things a little difficult.

Double proxy marriages do exist but they are hard to come by. One of the few places that does offer them is the American state of Montana. In fact they had such a booming market in double proxy weddings with couples applying from all over the world that it became a major problem. There were applications coming from as far away as China and Sweden and it was putting a great strain on the court services. The ceremony, which was normally a quick affair that only took around half an hour, was taking two hours or more as documents were being filled in incorrectly. The clerical staff were buckling under the strain, so a change in the law was put forward and now Montana's double proxy weddings are only available to serving members of the military. Since neither Collins nor Howard had been signed up for military service recently she would have to look elsewhere. Four other American states, California, Colorado and Texas also permit proxy weddings but they would only provide them for American citizens and insisted that one party showed up. Not many other countries were keen on providing the service or even recognising the marriage if you managed to get one.

But there are people on the internet who are happy to provide almost any service for a fee. For Collins this was her first exploration into the more dubious fringes of cyberspace but, as she would later do with hitmanforhire. net, when she found proxymarriages.com she jumped in feet first.

Proxymarriages.com no longer exists, like many of the websites mentioned in this story. The combined forces of legal and media scrutiny tend to persuade those involved in the less salubrious dealings online to vanish when the police come into view. If you go to the address now you find a polite notice telling you that 'this site is no longer active'. A discreet link leads you to nevadadivorce.net with the capitalised promise of 'Professional, Efficient and Low Cost Divorce and Annulment Services'. Proxymarriages. com was not one of the more reliable outfits. Despite the home page that promised 'Quick, legal double proxy marriages' the marriage certificate Collins eventually received was not worth the paper it was printed on. It was another example of her willingness to trust anyone who offered her her heart's desire, regardless of the small print. Not that proxymarriages.com had much small print. The site sported a stock photograph of a happy couple standing next to a white limo. In multicoloured text the home page trumpeted the long and illustrious history of the proxy marriage. But the paragraph that caught Collins's eye was the one that promised an alternative to Montana's new restrictions.

'Mexico and Paraguay also deal in mail-order proxy marriages. We arrange proxy marriages in Mexico or Paraguay. The average cost is $600 USD.

'Mexico has no residency requirements. Although expensive, from $500 to $800, a proxy marriage can be arranged in one day, without travel.

'Because of the current restrictive marriage laws, a number of Israeli couples are getting married by proxy or "mail-in" marriage through the consulate of Paraguay in Tel Aviv. According to Israeli law, the Interior Ministry must recognize and register these marriages.'

The site promised a no hassle procedure with downloadable forms and a list of documentation that needed to be provided. There was a price list dependent on how quickly you wanted to be a blushing bride. Collins baulked at the Emergency Marriage, promising for the knot to be tied within 72 hours and the marriage certificate in her hand within three business days. Besides, whichever package she eventually plumped for, she would have to pay an additional $450 to get it *apostilled* or certified for an English speaking court. She did want to get things sorted quickly though. She eventually settled on the more frugal ceremony which would take a week with the documents with her in seven working days. Taking into account the extra week it would take to get the marriage certificate translated and certified into English she could be Mrs Sharon Howard in as little as three weeks. Perfect! There was still a niggling doubt though. Just to be sure she fired off a quick email to the Mexican Embassy asking about proxy marriages. She soon got a reply but it wasn't quite what she was looking for. The girl at the Embassy was perplexed.

'I have never come across a proxy marriage in Mexico and I strongly doubt it would be possible.'

That was a bit of a problem but for some reason it didn't stop her. Sitting in Ballybeg House with the sleek grey laptop that Howard had bought to do his accounts before they'd moved the business into the business park, Collins sent in a tentative query to proxymarriages.com. She decided, to avert suspicion, to write as a couple in love but tangled up in complex circumstances. She sent one email from her own Eircom account but decided that

it wouldn't do for a correspondence. There was still the
risk that Robert or Niall would be checking something
on the reception computer at the office where her Eircom
account was set to log in automatically if you went onto
the Sign In page. They all used the internet in the office.
It was the only place that had usable speeds; the dial up
connection at the house was barely able to handle the most
basic of text based emails. It was too much of a risk to
have answers from proxymarriages.com popping up where
someone could get wind of what she was planning. But
she wasn't the only one who had an Eircom account.

P.J. Howard was not very technically minded and
didn't have much time for the internet. He used to leave
anything like online banking or booking flights to her.
The only email address he ever used was the one set up on
the office system. He never used the one that had been set
up for him when they'd got the dial up connection into
the house. But Collins knew his password. The emails she
sent to proxymarriages.com were from an idealised man
who would take charge of these things. A man who would
move heaven and earth to be married to her and who
would stamp his foot to get the service they deserved.

She started writing to Leonard@proxymarriages.com to
say that she just needed as much information as possible
before proceeding.

> 'What about inheritance? If one of us were to die we
> are worried about our respective children arguing
> whether the marriage actually existed.'

She explained that there was a 'great deal of opposition
to us getting legally married' so there was a necessity of

'keeping it from our families. It's a long story.' Because of this she explained would it be possible to send it to their solicitor rather than to their home. Leonard wrote back within a day. The marriage would take place in Mexico. It was all totally legal. They did dozens of double proxy marriages each year. Collins wrote back within hours. Would they have to physically go to Mexico? That might be difficult, if not impossible. Did Leonard know anyone who could go there as a witness? Leonard explained to her that the witnesses were provided and all she needed to do was to send original documents with the money and an extra $195 for any additional copies of the marriage certificate they would require.

It seemed like a good deal. Collins happily sent over her credit card details and agreed to the payment of $1,295 with the extra charge for the *apostille* translation and sent over all the necessary documentation. Apart from both their birth certificates there were other forms you could download from the website. They were a power of attorney to allow someone to stand in for the bride and groom for the Mexican ceremony and a simple contract giving the company the go ahead to proceed. The contract looked fair enough. The company even agreed to pay back 50% of the fee if the marriage wasn't accepted as legally binding. She already had a copy of Howard's birth cert not to mention his wife's death certificate and her own divorce certificate so getting certified copies for both of them wasn't a problem.

Collins realised that it could be problematic if the marriage certificate was delivered to her either at home or to the office. The envelope was likely to be large and Howard, or someone else taking a registered delivery, might be tempted to check what was inside. That was something she didn't want to have happen. As she had mentioned to Leonard, she would need to have it delivered somewhere else but maybe not her solicitor … it might be difficult to explain a marriage certificate even if she still hadn't given the guarantee of no marriage document yet. Then she remembered her old friend Matt Heslan. He wasn't a solicitor but an accountant was close enough. She'd known him for years, longer than she'd known Howard. He'd done book keeping for her when she'd had the shop and she had even invited him to the 'wedding' reception at Dromoland Castle. According to evidence given in court, she got in touch with him and explained the situation. She and Howard had needed to change their plans with the wedding. She made up a story and pretended that P.J. Howard's two sons had kicked up about it so they had to find a way around it. She told him about the proxy marriage explaining it was the only way they could be together. Would it be okay if she had the certificate delivered to his office? She could tell the legal people who were organising the marriage certificate that he was her legal representative. If the certificate was delivered to the house then the boys might get hold of it and she was worried what would happen if they found out they'd gone behind their backs. They might even destroy it. She would wait in for the delivery but she had promised Howard she would be with him in Spain around the time it was due to arrive.

Heslan had no idea about the fraud but agreed to help, so Collins got back in touch with Leonard and arranged for the certificate to be posted out there. Then she waited, and waited. The reception came and went. It was nearly

Christmas and there was still no sign of the marriage certificate. It was supposed to have taken a little over a week. Collins wrote back to Leonard, once again using Howard's email address.

> 'I have been trying to ring you several times in the past couple of weeks but the calls have been diverted to an answering machine. Sharon left a message over a week ago and again last night. I have to be honest with you I am getting worried and getting more sceptical as each day goes by. I need the date that the marriage ceremony took place.'

She pushed the point home with a bit of emotional blackmail.

> 'Sharon's passport is due for renewal soon and she had hoped to renew it in her married name.'

Then as a finishing touch she decided to make Howard a little bit hot tempered and ended on a threat with the fictional Collins the calming influence.

> 'The only thing stopping me contacting Paypal at the moment is Sharon but I can tell she's getting as worried as I am.'

It seemed to do the trick. Over the next few weeks she got all the forms and documentation sorted and was finally assured that the certificate was on its way to safe hands at Heslan's office. In the end he wasn't there when the certificate arrived. His secretary signed for it and put it in his office. Collins called round to the office a couple of days later and opened the official looking envelope right away. Inside were several documents. The original certificate, with its gold crest and elaborate purple border looked like something you'd knock up on the computer at home—but it had cost enough. It must have been valid. It gave the names P.J. Howard and Sharon Collins and said the ceremony had taken place in Trece in Mexico, which was nice to know. There was also a translation into English and a couple of other documents that seemed to be the certification, the mysterious apostille. Collins took the English copy of the certificate and thanked Heslan for his help, leaving the original with him for safety. Now she saw it she wasn't sure about the certificate. As always, late in the game, Collins started to worry she had been had. She needed to test whether it would stand up to official scrutiny, in case she ever needed it to when Howard wasn't around to be shocked.

She had been thinking about the best way to see if it worked. Well her passport had been in an unfortunate accident with a bottle of water. She couldn't possibly travel on it now, it was coming apart! Of course, she could have sent off for a replacement in her married name but on 22 February 2006, Collins travelled to the passport office in Cork. She had her birth certificate, her water soaked old passport and the Mexican marriage certificate. She filled out the passport form under the name Sharon Howard. She waited to go up to the counter then nervously handed over the small bundle of documents.

The girl behind the counter looked at them and then took them off to photocopy the certificates. Collins waited for her to say something about the marriage certificate but she nodded and gave her a receipt. They accepted it. It had worked! They would be sending her out a new passport with her married name in a couple of days. Now no matter what Howard and his sons thought, she was officially Sharon Howard. Now what could she do with that?

CHAPTER 5:

A HITMAN FOR HIRE?

It wasn't long before the new passport felt like it was burning a hole in her pocket. Collins had big plans now that she had a marriage certificate and a passport proving that she was Mrs P.J. Howard. So she hit the internet again some months after her 'marriage' looking for a way of disposing of any prying eyes who could put an end to her little game of make believe.

Towards the end of June 2006 the solution she hit upon was like it was straight out of a Cohen brothers' film. The idea that it was possible to order someone's murder from the comfort of your home, in perfect anonymity from start to finish, ensured that the proceedings in Court Number Two became the must-see entertainment for those who consider trial-watching a fun day out. But Collins wasn't considering getting caught when the idea came to her as she sat at the computer in Downes & Howard in August 2006. She knew you could get almost anything online. Why not this? It was quick, it was easy and, as long as she was careful, it was safe. It was the only way to go! Of course this time she couldn't simply use Howard's forgotten Eircom account. It wouldn't look very good if Howard were to order his own death—and also since the boys would need to be disposed of as well. No, there was no way she could use one of the Eircom accounts for this. This was something that needed a rather more impenetrable pseudonym. A web-based account would be best. Untraceable—or so she thought. So on 2 August she visited the web portal of Yahoo and signed up to it's free web mail service. Emboldened by the perceived anonymity she signed up as B. Lyons, the name of Howard's former partner, now deceased. Well, it wasn't as if Howard was going to see the emails so he wouldn't be put in a position to feel embarrassed or betrayed if she found what she was looking for. Now she needed an email address; something that suited her new role as a femme fatale. The old Eagles song kept weaving around her head.

> 'Ain't it funny how your new life didn't change
> things
> You're still the same old girl you used to be
> You can't hide your lyin' eyes.'

It was enough to make you cry. Well she wasn't going to be a victim. She had given up everything for him and for what? What if she had turned him down in 1998? What would her life be like now? Yahoo silently waited for a user name for her new account, an email address that suited the task in hand. There was only one choice really. The office was lunchtime quiet as she finally typed in the name Lyingeyes98. Done. She fiddled around for a bit before starting her search, testing the new account was actually working. She logged into her Eircom account and sent an email to Lyingeyes.

She couldn't help but ponder her situation. She hadn't expected the marriage certificate to look so ridiculously fancy. It looked nothing like an Irish marriage certificate. All that money wasted on a fake! She should have checked it was legal before she paid the money. Well she wouldn't make the same mistake this time.

Before she did anything else she checked out her situation once and for all, assuming that the Mexican certificate wasn't worth the paper it was written on. Citizens Advice sites and legal advisors weren't exactly encouraging. They all kept telling her same thing. She had no legal standing whatsoever. It was all very well him promising to set her up for life if they ever parted, but how would he feel if they actually broke up? What if it ended up badly? She would be homeless. It wasn't just her. She had to think of her sons. Howard had just helped David buy a house. What would happen to them if she walked out on him? She wouldn't do anything to harm her sons. What about if Howard passed away? With his heart there was always a chance, although he had been a changed man since he had had a bypass. He could end up outliving her. Even if he did die she would still have to depend on Robert and Niall to let her have what Howard had promised her. She'd been on at him for ages to put things on a more formal level and he'd promised to, but when it came down to it there was always something more important to do and he still hadn't gotten around to it.

She couldn't just wait and see how things panned out. She would have to take control. There had to be a way. Web searches for domestic violence didn't help much.

Howard wasn't violent and had never done anything to hurt her. She'd never be able to convince anyone she was a battered woman. She idly typed in alternate searches. Hire hitman; contract killer; assassin for hire. There were an impressive number of results. It made her wonder. Was it actually possible to find a hitman online? A real actual killer, sitting at his computer waiting for your call, ready to leap into action to do your bidding—so much more convenient that taking the trip to Limerick and having to deal with a killer face to face.

There were pages and pages of results when she typed in the terms. Most of them seemed to be referring to a computer game. That wasn't what she was looking for. Collins wasn't the familiar with the Hitman series of games. It's a popular franchise that's already spawned a film and countless chat rooms where obsessive gamers discuss tactics and cheat codes. But these sites were not going to be of any use whatsoever—unless of course one of the gamers could be persuaded to leave his bedroom for a couple of hours and put his marksmanship skills, learnt in front of his computer screen, to use. Probably not a good idea—that would be a different type of film script entirely. How do you find something other than that damn game? Collins varied the search terms she used. Hitman, Killer for hire, Assassin. There had to be something here. The afternoon was wearing on and she still hadn't found anything useful. In between the menial demands of typing and phone calls to be made she persisted in her search. Then she found it. Or thought she did anyway.

Hitman.us certainly looked like it meant business but unfortunately it wasn't the kind of business she had in mind. When Collins found the site she was greeted by a black screen. As she moved her mouse around a white circle appeared centred around a crosshair sight allowing glimpses of the home page beneath. She clicked through and the page was revealed showing a down turned handgun in a leather gloved hand with the page scattered with bullet holes. In discreet text at the bottom of the page the site promised;

'HITMAN offers a variety of assassination services and contract killing options. We are the industry leader in innovative killing techniques and manage a network of freelance assassins on five continents, available on short notice, around the clock. Next time you have a problem, remember: our contract killers are waiting for your call 24 hours a day, 7 days a week.'

A logo promised HITMAN – Professional Killings. The main home page of the site explained that the site offered the services of an independent outfit who could provide quick and efficient killings anywhere in the world for a fee of $50,000. They promised absolute professionalism and sure fire results. Collins wasn't familiar with the going rate for contract killers so the fee of $50,000 didn't seem exorbitant. The whole thing sounded so simple and efficient.

'Instead of fiddling around with amateur killing techniques and messing up crime scenes, just pick up the phone and give us a call. After reviewing your case, our team will develop a customized package that is best-suited for your particular situation. You provide us with the name of your mark, along with a photo and personal details, and take a vacation; we'll make sure one of our specialists sends flowers to the grieving widow while you enjoy your Marguerites on the beach.'

The website even offered discounts for three or more targets. It was just what she was looking for. They even accepted all major credit cards and gave gift certificates! Clearly tempted Collins sent off an email from the Lyingeyes address to the promising Hitman at killers@ hitman.us. But she was to be disappointed. Maybe she should have observed the little black and white rabbit at the foot of every page with the guarantee that 'Hitman is a cruelty free organization. None of our services have been tested on animals'. But Collins obviously didn't read that far down the page. So it was a bit of a disappointment when the automatic response came back.

'Please buy a HITMAN T-shirt from our online store.

PS—This site is not to be taken seriously. Thanks for looking.'

If she had looked around the site a bit more she could definitely have avoided any embarrassment. The testimonials suggest a somewhat dark sense of humour but no crack team of assassins.

'This guy moved in next door. I didn't like the way he looked in that shirt. So, I called HITMAN. I never saw him again. Or his shirt. Serves him right.'

Or;

'I was having a lot of problems with this jerk at work. Then I contacted HITMAN. Coincidentally, right around that time, our company organized a trip to the zoo. I was hardly able to contain my amusement next morning when I read the headline, "Terrified Onlookers Scream in Disbelief as Man Eaten Alive by Heard of Hungry Alligators". Due to the absence of a body the cops had to identify the victim by process of elimination. Needless to say, he never bothered me again. Thanks, HITMAN.'

If she had only read the disclaimer she would have been told that site was 'of course' a parody. Today, as a result of the unwanted attention the site received because of Collins's failure to read the small print, the disclaimer is a lot longer. Since the site owners learnt of their connection to a high profile Irish trial when they were contacted in the course of researching this book, they have decided to err on the side of caution and leave absolutely no doubt whatsoever that the site does not offer hits.

'First and foremost, we do not in any way promote, condone, encourage, advertise or otherwise endorse any kind of violence, crime or any kind of illegal activity, we do not engage, have never engaged in the past and will never engage in the future, in any kind of criminal or illegal activities, or any kind of endeavours that may be in violation of any laws, and we do not associate with any individuals that are involved (or have ever been involved) in any illegal or criminal activities.'

'To put it in simple English, we do not in any way offer any assassination services or any kind of services similar to that nature. The content published on our web site is written as a tongue in cheek joke and is to be read solely for its comical value.'

Hitman.us sells t-shirts and hoodies. In fact, it has sold t-shirts since it was set up in January 2005. They had never heard of Sharon Collins and were indignant at the perception, as presented by the Irish media and bloggers around the world, that they had emailed her and in some way played a part in the fiasco that was the game played by Lyingeyes and the contract killer she would later do business with.

'First of all, we did not send any emails to anyone in August 2006. In fact, we hardly ever send out any emails to anyone, from that email address, or regarding the hitman site at all. It would be very easy for anyone to fake their emails, and make them appear as if they were sent from any particular email address—and there is a remote possibility that someone did just that (i.e. that someone totally unrelated to us sent an email to the person in question and made it look as if it was sent from our email address). However, if that had been the case, then it would be safe to assume that the user in question would have sent a reply to that email address, and that reply would have come to us. But we never received any such replies.'

They went on to say that; 'Our site is a parody. We've always felt this was pretty obvious from the joking content of our descriptions. Anyone with the minimal level of intelligence can make the only reasonable conclusion that the site is not serious.'

Unfortunately it took Collins some time to realise the site was a spoof used to sell t-shirts. But it wasn't until after she had sent some emails that she realised this, and so the website address ended up as evidence for the prosecution during her trial. The email she had sent to killers@hitman. us was blurred with the evidence that was related to the site linked to her co-accused and there was no explanation of nature of the reply she received.

But when she realised this in August 2006 and the penny had finally dropped, she went back to her searches to find a hitman who would do the job and wasn't a character in a game or a device to sell clothing. Luckily for her, at around lunchtime on 3 March 2006, a 'Tony Luciano' had registered hitmanforhire.net. The site was registered to the Las Vegas address 4467 El Quinta, the address of the apartment Eid had set up with Engle. The contact phone number had been registered to Essam Eid. Much more basic in it's layout than hitman.us the sites had a lot in common on the surface; though hitmanforhire.net did not intend to sell t-shirts.

Ashraf Gharbeiah would later tell the FBI that Eid had asked him about setting up a website at around the time Engle was looking for someone to murder her husband. Gharbeiah didn't know anything about website design himself but he knew someone who did. Eid and Engle set up a meeting and within a couple of months hitmanforhire.net went live. When she took the stand in

Dublin, Engle described the website as a 'joke'. She smiled wryly as she told the court that she couldn't understand how anyone could take the site seriously. She didn't look at Collins as she described anyone who would fall for it as an 'idiot'. Certainly Collins had already proved her radar was faulty to say the least when it came to spotting dodgy websites and, just as with Proxymarriages.com the previous year, if the words 'Buyer Beware' weren't large and flashing on the home page Collins would accept its legitimacy without question. On 2 August 2006, in her second attempt to break into the internet underworld, she visited the site twice as she continued her quest to find a reliable contract killer online. While hitman.us trumpeted its credentials as a parody, hitmanforhire.net used a very similar model to apparently offer the service for real. Even though the website was so close to hitman.us it could be called a direct steal, the intention behind it was not to make people laugh. Though even now, it is difficult to say whether the site was genuinely offering the service it was pushing; if things had gone differently would a contract negotiated through the site actually have progressed to its planned conclusion?

It's not difficult to see Engle's point. The site, now defunct, was a lot less convincing than hitman.us. It had the appearance of having been done on the cheap. The home page with its blocky yellow script on a black background proclaimed that 'hitman for hire' was the 'perfect solution'. A graphic of an old school mobster loomed out of the black pointing a hand from the page. Acting as a flourish to the text that filled the body of the page and further underlining the promise of old school mafioso links was the image of a tommy gun. But there was nothing slick about the presentation of this site. Whoever had written the text for the site was obviously aware of hitman.us and had lifted from it liberally. Hitmanforhire. net showed the same brash confidence and made the same grandiose claims. The banner at the top of the home page promised the site was 'the perfect solution for all your killing needs.'

> 'We offer a variety of professional assassination services available worldwide. Whether you are trying to put an end to a domestic dispute or eliminate your business competitors, we have the solution for you.'

In a direct steal from the t-shirt shop they added;

> 'We are a privately-owned independent enterprise that specializes in reliable contract killings.
> We take our business very seriously and are the best at what we do.'

In fact, the text followed the other site's pitch very closely but somewhat more succinctly.

> 'Assassinations are the most practical solutions to common problems. Thanks to the internet, ordering a hit has never been easier. We manage a network of freelance assassins, available to kill at a moment's notice. All you have to do is send us an email, along with the details, and wait for further instructions. All the correspondence is done through our secure online forms.

'We offer several options to suit the specific needs of our clients. Each case is analyzed and designed for maximum protection and satisfaction.

'Basic contracts start at base cost plus expenses. We require a photograph, bio, and address of the target, along with a deposit. The balance is due no later than 72 hours after the job is done.'

Links led on to pages on How to Order, Secure Email and Employment. In smaller text at the very bottom of the screen there was even a disclaimer just like hitman. us but Collins didn't notice that one either. She was perhaps beginning to work out that everything you read online isn't necessarily so because, for once, Collins didn't go straight to How to Order. She played it a little bit cunning and filled in the employment form instead, to try to gauge whether this site was actually doing what it said it was doing. In keeping with her new found caution she used an alias. Not Bernie Lyons this time but a name even more impenetrable. Aware of the need to cover her tracks absolutely, Collins picked her own initial and her mother's maiden name, Cronin. Certainly no Mata Hari, Collins continued her high stakes subterfuge. In a flash of inspiration she typed in a made up phone number, they had the Lyingeyes address if they needed to contact her. She needed to find out about this quickly though. She had to find out where she stood. The best time to make contact was within the next 18 hours. Just to give them an idea what would be entailed, because the site seemed to be American, she helpfully gave her location as Ireland. No point in being any more specific until she knew she wasn't dealing with another joke.

She tried to answer the questions as truthfully as she could. After all she might be working with these people sometime in the near future. She didn't want them thinking she was one of them so she came clean and put 'none' by the heading 'Experience'. In a prophetic flash, she put down 'none yet' beside 'Criminal Record'. She didn't want to sound too virtuous though, you never knew with these Americans, so beside 'Skills', a category which covered firearms, explosives, poisons, martial arts or torture she volunteered a skill with a hand gun.

After a while, when no reply was fired back telling her it was all a legitimate joke, she contacted the site again using the 'Secure Email' form. Once again she gave the name Cronin, but this time she provided her mobile number as well as the Lyingeyes address. It was time to put her cards on the table.

> 'Two male marks in Ireland, usually together. Make it look like an accident. Then possibly another one within 24 hours, preferably like suicide. Would appreciate a call by return.'

She had taken the bait. Now all 'Tony Luciano', the man who ran the site, had to do was reel her in.

Hitmanforhire.net was not an original idea. The internet has always been an ideal breeding place for scams and even more sinister transactions to propagate. In an environment where porn is always around the next corner and the legal and illegal rub shoulders with perfect ease, it's hardly surprising that the idea of the killer for hire had found its way online. In 2008 the FBI warned about a wide spread email scam in which the conman would announce himself as someone hired to carry out a hit on the unfortunate recipient of the email. This email, which has turned up in inboxes across the States and as far afield as the UK and Australia, would warn against any attempt to contact the law. 'You are being watched,' it warned. 'We will know if you do anything to try and trace us'. Like the 'Tony Luciano' scam, a demand is made for money to cancel the hit but this scam lacks the personal touch. While more aggressive than many other so-called phishing scams, the hitman emails are no different from the missives from so-called Lotteries or deposed African dignitaries who need your bank details to shift their millions out of a country. For some people though, the added threat was enough to make them part with thousands and for the emails to spark the attention of the FBI.

Hitmanforhire.net also wasn't the only site that tried to take the scam to another level. In amongst the joke sites there are one or two that are almost what they seem to be. Like hitmanforhire.net they usually hit the headlines when the people behind them are finally fingered by the law. In 2004 a Vietnamese student came to the attention of the authorities in Seoul when the 'hitman for hire' website he had set up to pay off a €1,100 loan became a little too successful. He was arrested after receiving a little over €5,500 from a young woman who wanted her ex and his new girlfriend taken care of. The case had startling similarities to the hitmanforhire.net case, even down to the charges the various parties faced. Given the timing of the 2004 case it's even possible that the hitmanforhire.net conspirators had been aware of the earlier website, maybe even inspired by it when it made headlines in the States.

The received wisdom garnered from forums and message groups would appear to suggest that anyone actually offering themselves as a killer for hire, anyone who knows what they are doing at least, does not set out their stall in such an obvious fashion. Hitmen do not tend to tout for business with three for two offers. The mercenaries that genuinely offered their services on a Mexican small ads site, for example, were far more matter of fact than the grandiose claims you could find on hitmanforhire. net. They were also a lot cheaper than the $50,000 asking price that was charged. But for Collins and the others who entered into correspondence with 'Luciano' skulking around the classifieds just didn't fit with the image they had of assassins. Collins wasn't alone in taking the site at face value.

For a site that was so obviously a 'joke' the take up rate wasn't bad. At least two other people had also filled out that application form and only one of them seemed to share Engle's view that hitmanforhire.net wouldn't fool anyone. One of them was Private Brian Buckley, a member of the Irish Defence Forces, who thought the site was a joke. When he took the stand in June 2008, Private Buckley seemed perplexed at all the fuss. He told the court room with absolute sincerity that he had never once thought the site was anything other than a joke …even when he started getting phone calls asking him to kill people. When he stumbled across hitmanforhire.net in the summer of 2006, 21-year-old Buckley was living with his mother in Ennis, Co. Clare. Having joined the army at the age of nineteen, Buckley had recently returned from a six month tour of duty in Liberia and was enjoying some time at home. He certainly wasn't looking for an opportunity for a little bit of moonlighting. Buckley was a clean cut young man with a strong Dublin accent, revealing his Finglas roots. Sitting at the computer in his mother's house on 29 July he was simply looking for cheat codes to unlock the hidden possibilities of his computer game. Buckley was a fan of the Hitman series of games, the same games Collins would have come across when she searched Yahoo for an affordable assassin. On that summer's afternoon in 2006 Buckley typed the word 'hitman' into his browser. Among the results he got was a website promising the services of a certain 'Tony Luciano'. Buckley had to have a look.

A cursory look around hitmanforhire.net confirmed his opinion that this was indeed one of the many joke sites that had popped up around cyberspace. As a joke he decided to fill out the application form, just as Collins had done. Unfortunately for Buckley he didn't come across as a secretary. He was curious to see where the site led so he provided the email address he had created to keep in touch with family and friends while he was away in Liberia: judas69@gmail.com. In another attempt at anonymity he created the pseudonym 'Will Buckimer' then he got into the spirit of the 'joke'. Unlike Collins's somewhat prophetic modesty, Buckley filled in details that exaggerated his abilities and skills. He gave himself an extra two years experience and beefed up his military prowess considerably. For a teenager who had only served with the Irish army on neutral peace keeping duties he volunteered a long list of martial skills, some of which actually existed. According to the application form on hitmanforhire.net, Buckley was a dab hand at 'handgun, rifle, sub-machine gun, shotgun, sniper rifle, heavy gun, heavy machine gun, grenades, basic booby traps and limited poisons'.

He would later tell the court, full of bored reporters giddy with the heat of the heavy summer afternoon that 'heavy gun' and 'heavy machine gun' weren't actually real weapons. Just as well then, that the people on the other end of the website weren't skilled tacticians and didn't notice this faux pas. Buckley seemed like a promising applicant with his promise 'You got work? I'll do it,' he even explained that his employment objective was 'to make money'. But back in the summer of 2006 Buckley filled in the form and forgot about it, the mild curiosity about what the punch line of the bizarre game was could be forgotten as he found the cheat codes and got back to his Hitman game.

However, a little over a week later he got a reply he wasn't expecting. 'Tony Luciano' had sent him a mail.

> 'Thanks for your email. Are you available? What's your phone number? We can contact you. Thanks. Tony Luciano.'

Buckley was perplexed. As a punch line this wasn't much good. The sneaking suspicion that the website the other week hadn't actually been a joke didn't start nagging just yet. So he replied to the mafia sounding 'Luciano' with his real name and mobile number. Then the next day a second email arrived.

'I have a job for you if you are interested. Two
male[s] in Ireland and one in Spain A.S.A.P. Let us
know. We will try to call you.
Thanks.
Tony Luciano'

Still Buckley was trying to see the joke. It was an odd
one all right. It really wasn't that funny. Then a couple
of days later his phone rang in the middle of the night.
Answering the phone in the middle of the night and
hearing a heavily accented male voice introduce itself as
Tony, Buckley most likely wondered what was really going
on. When the phone rang again, Buckley insisted he didn't
know any Will Buckimer. They must have the wrong
number. He didn't know anything about a 'Tony Luciano'
or any hitman website. But 'Luciano' wasn't giving up and
rang twice more in the middle of that night. Eventually
the phone calls stopped. Buckley finally got to sleep and
tried not to think anymore about the dodgy characters
that hung around odd corners of the internet. He seemed
to have got rid of the 'Luciano' guy. There were certainly
no more calls. Over the next few days, Buckley began to
think maybe the joke had been on him all along.

Unknown to him 'Tony Luciano' had been busy. By
the time he had rung Buckley on 16 August, Collins had
been well and truly reeled in and had sent €15,000 in a
Fed Ex parcel addressed to Teresa Engle at the home she
was now sharing with Essam and Lisa Eid, 6108 Camden
Cove Street. The plan was progressing rapidly and by 29
August Engle was ready to fly to Ireland to check out
the marks. It was time to contact judas69 again. Buckley
finally realised that hitmanforhire.net was not the joke it

seemed when he received an email on the day Engle was due to fly out.

> 'Hello Brian. Please help us out for this. I need some strong poison. One of us will be there at Shannon 7.20 a.m. tomorrow coming from the States and we can't ship this stuff for security reason[s]. You know that so please help us out. We will pay and I will owe you a favour. Thanks brother. Tony.'

Buckley did not like what he was hearing and had no intention of doing anything wrong. This was all getting far too dodgy. He stopped answering his phone to the late night calls and didn't reply to any more emails. The request for poison had made him feel uneasy but he still doubted that he had managed to contact someone who was capable of carrying out a contract killing; after all, he had thought 'hitman' was merely a computer game. There was something about that website that just didn't ring true. He assumed the website was some sort of parody.

Buckley wasn't alone in thinking hitmanforhire.net was a joke. A search of the various kinds of online chatter from around that time shows that hitmanforhire.net had been noticed in the forums and blogs around the world. Frequently suggested as a humorous solution to the many irritations wandering around cyberspace 'Tony Luciano's' sales pitch was the subject of several discussions arguing whether or not the company behind the Hitman computer game was attempting a bizarre publicity stunt.

But there were others who contacted hitmanforhire. net that never once thought it was a joke. Collins was not the only one who filled out that online application form. There was another shadowy figure who also made contact. He could have been another fantasist or a joker keen to take the gag to its furthest limits but 'John Smith' seemed ready to prove the skills with which he had fleshed out in his CV. John Smith called himself 'No Risk'. When he wrote to 'Luciano' in early August 2006 he was confident in his abilities as a poisoner.

> 'Tony, accidents happen … to other people. They eat things that don't agree with them and people die from food poisoning all the time. I have made my own and purchased others—personal favourite is blowfish bladder. My express is CMD with 101st. Tactical removal. Also Nicotine, Dioxine, cyanide or Sarin, depends on the dosage and delivery method as to timing. If you have specific needs please let me now and it WILL happen that way. I didn't come to the dance to sit and watch, Brother. I want to dance. What do you say?'

On 15 August he suggested a more down to earth prescription option, rather than the outlandish blowfish venom.

> 'Ouabain. 0.002 gms of ouabain is a lethal dose fore and [sic] adult human. If you prefer a cardiac glycosidene e.g. digitalis. Slow the heart right down. Increase the cardiac output. Increase the cardiac enlargement and decrease venous pressure by working on the vagus nerve. Painful and effective and I could make it out of Oleander or Milkweed.'

John 'No Risk' Smith helpfully provided the correct dosage, which was duly parroted back to Collins as a possible means of dispatching Howard's two sons. He might even have been a suitable accomplice for Engle's first trip to Ireland, sounding suitably desperate as he wrote to 'Luciano' on 19 August;

'Tony, I could really use this contract. Call me in the morning. Lets talk it over.'

He sounded almost plaintive when he emailed again.

'I would like to get this resolved today if that's possible. I have a personal matter that I need to clear up this weekend. I am not trying to be picky or seem impatient. I am ready to go and as I said I would like to clear up an issue I have. Call me or email me your reply.'

'Luciano' did get back to him. This was a relationship that both sides were keen to develop in a professional way.

'Ok Brother, I have to give you this but can you do it for $10,000 plus expenses. We will pay you the ticket and give you $2,000 dollars expenses for two days in Ireland. I will take the other guy out and I will take the last for the money that I had home. Can you do it or not? No neg if yes or no, let me know. If yes you have to go there Friday, August 25th and the job will be done by Saturday, August

26th. Let us know. I will take care of you next time. Please. Thanks. Tony.'

But 'Smith' wasn't impressed with the fee. If he had known the figure that 'Luciano' had hammered out with Collins he would have been even more reluctant.

'Well Tony. Send the boys and call me Saturday around noon some time. We can work out the details then. 10 stick a little shorter than I expected but I will take you at your word. Give me all details in the business. I will talk to you soon.'

He reminded 'Luciano';

'Our job makes trust difficult. Don't want unwelcome visitors at my door you understand. Call me, lets talk or tell me what exactly you need.'

But in the end helpful 'Smith' did not join Engle in Ireland and the conspirators decided to try some home brew poisons of their own. 'John Smith' himself faded back into the shadows of cyberspace. He was not a witness in the trial of Sharon Collins and Essam Eid.

So hitmanforhire.net was ticking over nicely and had succeeded in attracting the attention of some very interested customers. Until the conspirators decided to dabble in a bit of practical chemistry, hitmanforhire.net was in position as an almost perfect con. If Engle and Eid had satisfied themselves with corresponding with the desperate women who had contacted the website they could have made a pretty satisfactory turn over. As a scam, the hitman website was almost perfect. The best mark, after all, is the one with the most to lose. Who would dare to blow the whistle to the cops when it would mean admitting a plot to dispatch their nearest and dearest? If those behind the website had been content with simply gathering enough money from deposits, they wouldn't even have to leave their house, never mind carry out a hit. But the gamblers saw a chance to win twice and so their scam came crashing down around them. While the person arranging the hit might be slow to come forward and admit they had been scammed, the supposed target has no similar constraint. Eid and Engle made this mistake both times someone approached the hitmanforhire.net website, for Collins was not the only one who came looking for someone to be bumped off.

While Collins was flirting with 'Luciano' and whispering sweet nothings during late night phone calls as she plotted her inheritance, somebody else had come looking for psychopathic expert help. Eid and Engle ended up double jobbing, getting caught for one job just days before they set off to confront Robert and Niall Howard.

Marissa Mark had come across hitmanforhire.net while trawling through the internet just like Collins. Marissa had been getting over a break up when she stumbled upon hitmanforhire.net which promised to be 'the perfect solution'. She would tell her ex when he phoned her wanting to know why a strange couple had just turned up threatening to shoot his new girlfriend in the head that she too had thought hitmanforhire.net was a joke and had put the unfortunate love rival's details in just for a laugh.

Even though no one was charged with conspiring to murder anyone in this particular case, the similarities with what was going on in Ireland at much the same time are striking. Eid and Engle took a contract forged through hitmanforhire.net and decided to maximise their profits. Just as they demanded money in late September 2006 from Robert Howard they approached the woman Marissa had joked about having killed and asked her to buy herself out of the contract.

CHAPTER 6:

CALIFORNIA OR BUST

When Marissa Mark contacted hitmanforhire.net she was looking for someone to heal the pain of a break-up.[1] It was almost a year since she had broken up with her boyfriend of three years, Joshua. When she had heard he'd left Pennsylvania to try his luck in show business and had moved in with his new girlfriend, she was upset. She didn't mind if Joshua wanted to be a singer. She'd never stood in his way. Even after they split up she would go and see him perform in his stage persona as 'Monte Carlo'. She'd even travelled all the way to Philadelphia to watch him record. But moving away into the arms of another woman? That hurt.

Jealously drove Marissa to do the unthinkable and send an email to hitmanforhire.net. She already had some information on her former boyfriend's new girlfriend. It was so easy to snoop about his new life. Both he and his new flame had Myspace pages. It was just a coincidence that his profile was deleted at the same time he was moving in

---

1   Evidence given in the trial of Teresa Engle heard before the Californian Central District Court, USA.

with her! A visit to the recording studio had been an ideal opportunity to copy his phone contacts, after all, they even had the same make of mobile phone. You can find out so much about a person online. You can also find solutions to a lot of problems while you're at it. Like Collins, when Marissa stumbled upon hitmanforhire.net it seemed to provide the ideal answer to her problems. Whether she thought of it as a joke is not known, but she filled in her love rival's details and entered into a correspondence with 'Luciano'. In her quest to find out exactly who Joshua had hooked up with, she had found quite a lot of information about Anne Lauryn Royston. Marissa had allegedly taken photos from Royston's Myspace page and had all the details about where she worked as a loan broker.[2] She sent the info to 'Luciano'.

Of course, 'Luciano' wouldn't be shooting anyone. Instead of a sharp Italian hitman it was Eid and Engle who turned up at Royston's office on 15 September 2006. She had received a phone call from Eid three days earlier. He had spun a line about wanting to refinance the house in Las Vegas and said someone had recommended that he speak to her. He would be in Santa Rosa, California, he said, would it be possible to meet there? Royston told him she had no idea where Santa Rosa was but she could meet him somewhere in between. Eid called her back later that day and changed the arrangement. He told her he and his wife would be in their hotel in Beverly Hills on Saturday, 16 September, they could meet Royston at around 8.30 a.m. On the morning of the 16th, Royston decided that

---

2   Evidence given in the trial of Teresa Engle heard before the Californian Central District Court, USA.

meeting at the hotel wasn't the best idea so she rang Eid on his mobile and told him to meet her in the office at 10 a.m. At 9 a.m. he rang her back and asked her what was taking her so long. He was already at the office. His yellow Corvette was an exceptionally fast way of getting from A to B. Royston told him she would still be arriving at 10 a.m. Why didn't he wait for her?

Arriving at the office she looked around but didn't see any yellow Corvette. Of course he might be parked somewhere out of sight. She headed upstairs to her office to prepare for the meeting. A few minutes later, Eid and Engle were let into the building by the receptionist. Royston met them at the lift and brought them into the conference room. That was when that ordinary Saturday morning took a turn and things started to get very weird indeed. Royston sat down at the conference table with Eid sitting opposite her. Engle closed the door behind them and went and sat down in a chair up against the wall. She didn't say much during the meeting.

It was Eid who did all the talking.[3] The two of them were dressed head to toe in black. Eid was looking every inch the gangster with his thick moustache, black suit and black dress shirt. When he arrived he was wearing his trademark metal aviator sunglasses. Engle sat quietly, wearing black trousers and a long sleeved black shirt. Royston noted the smell of cigarette smoke that came into the room with her and that when she opened her mouth to speak her teeth were badly stained with nicotine. Royston tried to get the meeting underway. She handed Eid a package showing all

---

3   Evidence given in the trial of Teresa Engle heard before the Californian Central District Court, USA.

the details for the loans the company offered. Eid looked at it briefly before pushing it back to her. He brought out a folder of his own and pushed it across the table towards Royston. She looked at the black zip up folder lying in front of her. It was full of photographs of her. She recognised them immediately. They were the ones from her Myspace page. She looked at Eid in shock. He calmly looked back at her and told her,

'Somebody wants your head. Somebody wants you killed and they hate you a lot.'

Royston was stunned and upset. She started crying. Eid allegedly pulled out an email sent from Marissa's email address.[4] It said that Marissa had put down a deposit of $17,000 and wanted Royston shot in the head. Royston was terrified. She had already received strange phone calls from a woman who had told Royston in no uncertain terms to stay away from her man. Joshua, who had been living with her since he had moved up to L.A. a couple of weeks ago, was sure that Marissa was behind that call. Now this? What on earth had she done now? Eid leaned forward and told her that it was going to be all right. Royston reminded him of his daughter. He couldn't bring himself to kill her. Royston listened carefully.

Unfortunately there was a problem, Eid told her. If he didn't follow through on the contract there was nothing to stop Marissa getting someone else who would carry out the killing. But there was a way out. He could always get rid of Marissa for her. Then there would be no one to come after her. No! Royston didn't want anything to do

---

4   Evidence given in the trial of Teresa Engle heard before the Californian Central District Court, USA.

with another plot and she certainly had no reason to want Marissa dead. She ran out of the conference room in tears. Eid and Engle stayed sitting there. Royston's colleagues gathered around her trying to find out what was wrong.

'Those two people in the conference room … they're not clients. They want to kill me!'

Gathering herself together she went back into the conference room to face them. Her assistant, Melanie Kasemaier went in with her for moral support. Royston told Eid she couldn't give him any kind of answer today. She needed to talk things through with her boyfriend. Eid was understanding. They could come back at 11.30 p.m. once she had talked things over with Joshua; when she'd had a chance to think through her situation. Kasemaier, taking in the conman's appearance and the folder of photographs on the table asked Eid if he was for real. 'Yes, sweetheart', he replied, as he and Engle stood up to leave. As he left the conference room Eid went over to Royston and gave her a big hug to say goodbye.[5]

As soon as they had left Royston emailed Joshua. He didn't answer her straight away. He was still getting settled in L.A. and had gone to a job fair that morning. He was in an interview when his phone beeped. He didn't look at it. Royston kept emailing him as the enormity of what she had just been through began to hit. By the time Joshua looked at his phone there were a stack of messages. He realised she needed help and headed straight over to her office. Royston was still frantic when he arrived. She told

---

5   Evidence given in the trial of Teresa Engle heard before the Californian Central District Court, USA.

him about the visit from Eid and Engle. The criminals had claimed that Marissa sent them.

'She wants me dead!'

She told him about the email Eid had showed her and how it said that Marissa had paid $17,000 to have her shot in the head. They were coming back, she told him. Joshua tried to make her call the cops but she was too scared. They could still be around. She didn't even want to leave the safety of her office.

Joshua was determined to get to the bottom of things. He rang Marissa who denied everything.

'What are you talking about? I never hired any hitman.'[6]

Joshua told her he just wanted to know the truth. Had she hired someone to kill Royston as the email had suggested? Marissa denied everything. Royston grabbed the phone out of Joshua's hand. Marissa wasn't going to tell her anything. The conversation degenerated and Marissa announced that she had been pregnant with Joshua's baby only three months ago, although she wasn't pregnant any more. In her anger and frustration Royston hung up. She just couldn't listen to any more. A few seconds later Joshua's phone beeped again. It was a text from Marissa. She hadn't hired any hitman. Someone had probably hacked into her computer and sent those mails. A strikingly similar defence to the one that Sharon Collins would be using in court the following year.

It was now almost 11.30 p.m. Royston didn't want the hitman and Engle turning up again so she called Eid. He

---

6   Evidence given in the trial of Teresa Engle heard before the Californian Central District Court, USA.

told her to meet him at a place called Cables Restaurant in the Woodland Hills area but when she and Joshua drove up they couldn't see either Eid or Engle anywhere around the restaurant. Royston called Eid again. The restaurant had been far too crowded for the conversation they needed to have, he told her, and he was waiting for her in the Holiday Inn just down the street. Sure enough, when Joshua pulled up in front of the Inn, Engle was sitting on a bench outside waiting for them. She got up to meet them and curtly told them to follow her. She led them through the lobby of the hotel to the pool area in the back. She sat down at a patio table and gestured for them to join her. Joshua was nervous, constantly checking the surrounding roofs for a sniper trained on them as they sat there.

Engle lit a cigarette and pushed an email towards them. Joshua saw that the mail was from thenotebuyer@yahoo.com but he recognised the style as being that of Marissa's.[7] She was talking about a contract on Royston's life and calmly discussed prices. He noticed Engle's hands were skinny with prominent veins. Her fingers were nicotine stained. As she spoke, he also noticed her teeth were stained and decayed. Her shoes were open toed and he thought she could have done with a pedicure.

Pulling himself together he asked Engle what they were going to do to sort out the situation. You've two choices, she told him. Either your girlfriend dies or the two of you get the money together to pay the balance on the contract. If they didn't come up with the $37,000 by 29 September

7   Evidence given in the trial of Teresa Engle heard before the Californian Central District Court, USA.

something could still happen to Royston. She then turned to Royston.

'You're the luckiest woman in America,' she told her. 'Normally we don't allow the mark a way out.'

She said they normally just handled the matter and didn't give the mark a chance. Joshua told her there was no way they could get that kind of money. Engle looked at him across the table.

'Is that what you'll say when Lauryn is buried next Tuesday?'

Royston wanted to talk to Eid but Engle told her he wasn't around at the moment. He'd be in touch though. She got up to leave. Royston and Joshua didn't see Eid at all that time, but as they were driving away from the Holiday Inn they spotted Engle waving at a yellow Corvette. As they drove away Joshua rang Marissa again. He told her he'd just been reading the emails she had sent to the hitman. He said she would go to jail for this.[8] Marissa started crying. She never meant any harm. She was sorry. It had all been a joke that had gotten out of hand.

A few days later, Royston got a phone call from a man calling himself 'Tony Luciano'. She recognised the Middle Eastern accent. She was sure it was really Eid. She asked 'Luciano' how she could trust him. How could she know that Marissa wouldn't just go and hire a different hitman? 'Luciano' told her not to worry. He knew the business he said. He came from a family of hitmen, in fact his father ran the biggest network of assassins in the United States. If anyone was trying to hire a replacement they would know

---

8   Evidence given in the trial of Teresa Engle heard before the Californian Central District Court, USA.

about it. Once she had paid off 'Luciano' it would all be over. She would never hear from them again. She later told Joshua about the call and he finally managed to convince her to go to the police. But by the time the arm of the law stretched out in the direction of Eid and Engle they had come into contact with the law in Ireland after upping their game considerably and trying to net the big one. Eid rang Royston on 19 September, a week after turning up at her offices. On the 26th he was standing on Robert Howard's doorstep trying to make him an offer he couldn't refuse. In both cases though, the offers were refused.

CHAPTER 7:

LYING EYES AND TONY LUCIANO

At the beginning of August 2006, Collins took the plunge and sent off the first tentative email to hitmanforhire.net At around quarter to four on Tuesday, 8 August, sitting in the front office at Downes & Howard she sent off her request.

> 'Two male marks in Ireland. ASAP. Usually together. Must look like accident. Then possibly a third within 24 hours. Prefer a suicide. Would appreciate a call by return.'

It didn't take long for 'Luciano' to get back to her. Almost by return he fired back.

> 'I got your email. We will call you within 30 minutes. Can you email us back with more info before we call?'

True to his word he called. Collins hadn't provided the information he asked for at first. For once she was being careful. But soon after she put the phone down she was at the keyboard again.

'Hi. We were just talking. As you can imagine I am extremely nervous about sending this message and even talking on the phone.

There are actually three, but two of them would probably be together and the third would not be in Ireland, he would be in Spain.

The first two live in Ireland as I said. The town they live in is Ennis, Co. Clare, in the west of the country. They are brothers. One aged 27 (big guy) and 23 (not so big). They share a house at present but there are two others living in the house as well.

They work in the same place and spend a lot of time together. I do not want it to look like a hit. This is important. I want it to look like an accident—perhaps travelling in a car together or in a boat (they do a lot of boating) off the west coast. Or maybe you have some ideas of you own.

The third is an older man—aged 57 and not very fit or strong. He would probably be in mainland Spain if not in Ireland. His location would depend on when the job could be done. Again it is imperative that it does not look like a hit. I would prefer suicide—or is it possible for it to look like natural causes? He's got a lot of health problems.

What I need to know is:

1: How soon could the above be done? Days, weeks, months?

2: If the first job is done in Ireland, is it possible for the second job to be done within 12 to 24 hours in Spain if that's where he is?

3: How much would it cost and how much of a deposit would be needed up front? I ask this because I would have no problem getting my hands on the money immediately afterwards but it certainly would be very tricky beforehand.

4: Can it be done in the manner I've stated—without causing suspicion?

5: Most importantly, if a deposit must be paid how do I know that you would not disappear with the money and not do the job? After all who could I complain to?

6: Where are you located? Just curious about that!

It might be easier to email back for now. I'm not comfortable talking about it on the phone—even though this phone is unregistered and not used for anything else. I may get a chance to email you again within the next hour but I will be tied up tomorrow for approximately three days.'

Collins was being careful, as careful as she had ever been in an internet transaction. She remembered the hassle of getting the Mexican marriage certificate and was determined not to make the same mistakes ... besides; it didn't hurt to be thorough. She was as truthful as she could be. There was no point in hiding anything. She would indeed be unavailable for the next three days. Her embryonic career as a femme fatale would have to go on hold while she made her yearly trip to the prayer retreat at

Lough Derg. She wouldn't have to wait the three days to hear back from her hitman though. 'Luciano' didn't take long to reply. This was definitely looking promising.

'I got your email and I agree with you about the phone and every time you email me delete it. I will email you tonight and give you an answer. We have people all over the world, in Ireland and in Spain too. Just take a day to contact them. If not I have people from the UK too so now that's my problem not you[rs]. I will contact you ASAP. Let you know all the info. But the most we have to trust each other. If these people [are] related to you, don't contact them and go away from them …'

A few hours later he was back, having checked an imaginary Filofax.

'Hello. Well we discuss about you[r] situation and we assume that these people is your two stepsons and your husband. Maybe we are right and maybe we are wrong. It's important to know that to protect you and protect ourself too. For your safety if that so we can do two male first and after cool off we will do the third one. If that right tell us who the most beneficial to you we can do it first.

Now for all your question that you ask us earlier. Our price per person is $50,000 USD but cause three bird in one stone it will be $90,000 USD. Before we start we have to have a deposit of $45,000. You have a choice of Fedex money order or cashier cheque or you can transfer the money to our bank.

If we agree we can finish our job Saturday, August 19. Either one of them the two guys or the third person.

When we get the money we will process and our experience do what['s] the best for both party. You get you money back if we are failed or we didn't do the job. But if you cancelled, your deposit is non-refund. I guess we answer all your questions. Just tell us more info about our target.

Thanks,

Tony Luciano'

Anxious to seal the deal he wrote again a short while later, forgetting the time distance and the fact that Collins would be unavailable for the next three days.

'Let me know if you got our message ... if you agree or not.'

But Collins was out of reach for the time being. 'Luciano' passed the time trying to convince Private Buckley to lend a helping hand. Buckley, of course, was never going to do anything wrong and had no idea about what Collins was planning with her American conspirators. However, three days later, true to her word, Collins was back.

'Hi Tony,

Yes I got your message but only just now—I've been away and had no access to the internet. Obviously at this stage, I realise you probably wouldn't be able to get the job done by August 18th.

Anyway, you are right about my relationship to the men in question. I know it must seem terrible of me but my back's to the wall and I don't have much choice. I would prefer it if it was just my husband, but because of the way he has arranged his affairs it would be way too complicated if his sons were still around and I'd still be in much the same situation as I am now.

Regarding payment. The price you quoted seems very fair and I would gladly pay it, but I will have to give some thought on how to come up with the deposit. I could put my hand on it, in cash, immediately but the two sons would see it gone and would know it was me and that would cause too many problems for me. I'll have to try to borrow it and that will take a little time. I'm not even sure that I will get it—I don't have any assets of my own to borrow against, but I'll certainly give it a go.

Now you said in your message that you'd leave a cooling off period between the first two and my husband. How long were you thinking of? I'll tell you the way I was thinking. My husband is in Spain and lives on the top floor of a tall building while he's there. If he were to hear that his sons had a fatal accident he might suddenly feel suicidal and just jump off the building. Is that too far fetched do you think? Otherwise he would find out about the missing money (if I try using that) and if I borrow it from the local bank (the only place I'd have a chance of getting it) he'd hear that too and put two and two together. It's very parochial here. My husband is very friendly with the bank manager and they talk a lot. Another thing I'll have to look into is the cashier's cheque or bank draft. There's a record kept here of anything over a certain amount —I'm not sure if its 5K or 10K but I assume I could send a few drafts. I'd be worried that if the cops got suspicious though and looked into it, I wouldn't have any answers. Do you know if cash can be parcelled up and FedExed safely?

I have to go to Spain next week—my husband is putting me under pressure to join him and I must try to keep him happy for now, while I figure things out.

You quoted in USD so I assume the money goes to the US and then the guy or guys doing the job get their cut from there. I'm saying this, just in case it would be possible to give you the location of cash to be picked up after each job is done. Is there any chance of that, do you think? It would be very uncomplicated for me in that situation. I could go ahead with it straight away.

The other thing I need to know is if it's possible for it to look like an accident and not a hit?

I look forward to hearing from you. S.'

'Luciano' lost no time in replying and set about reeling her in. The conspiracy, after all, was all about money.

'We have already reservation at hotel called Greenhills at Ennis Rd, Limerick the 18 August but we will do it the 19. We decide to send two women and a man to do that job and I will do third one myself in Spain. We will poison the two guys. We will use the two women to get close to them. About the money, you can't send cash but you can get to any other bank not your[s] and make [a] cashier cheque and send it. And we have to have deposit before I give my order to my people to do the job. I'm here in the US but my people, the man [is] from Germany and one woman from Ireland and other woman [from] Romania. If you have any question email me or I can call you if you want.

Thanks.

Tony Luciano.'

Collins now committed herself to ordering the murders and sent the would-be killers details they would require.

'Thanks for getting back to me so fast. Wow. I'm a bit scared to be honest.

The two guys here usually go to a place called Kilkee, on the west coast of Clare, each weekend. They've got a holiday home there. They usually have friends with them and the younger one usually has his girlfriend with him. The older guy (27) broke up with his girlfriend a couple of months ago and might be open to being chatted up etc. I think he has been dating lately but I don't know yet if he might bring that girl with him. I can find out but it will be Monday before I see him. It would be too suspicious for me to ring him over the weekend to ask.

They drink in a bar called the Greyhound Bar on the main street in Kilkee. It's easy to find. What do you plan? Putting poison in their drinks? I have to ask you what poison it would be—autopsies would be done and I need to know what they would be concluded from the autopsies. I think it might be easier for your people to stay in a hotel in Kilkee and get talking to them in the bar, but then you know you[r] business—I don't.

I would be in Spain with my husband when the above job would be done, if it's arranged for next weekend or even after that. What would you do about him? Especially with me around. You say you will take care of him yourself. You'd be coming a long way from the US to Spain. I could get the keys of his apartment to you and arrange a time to be out. I would be a suspect if anything looks suspicious, especially when I would be the one to inherit. Many people think I'm with him for his money anyway—he's a bit older than me etc and that would also look suspicious.

Please realise that I may not be ready to go ahead as soon as next week. I'm leaving here to go to Spain on Wednesday and it will take a lot longer than that for me to arrange a loan. I won't be back in Ireland until some time in September—it may be toward the end of the month before I'm back.

You see, as I said, I could use cash that I have here and buy a cashier's cheque, or a number of them, but the sons might notice the money gone after I leave on Wednesday and ring my husband and tell him. And he would know that I took it. And then what? This is my problem and I will have to work it out. But as I say, it might not be as soon as I hoped. I'd really like to see an end to all this soon, though.

I can't talk on the phone right now and I will be away from the computer for the next few hours. You could always send a text to my mobile phone but it would be better for now to send an email.

I appreciate all your help and we will definitely do business. I've no conscience about my husband, he's a real asshole and makes my life hell, but I do feel bad about the others. However, I thought about it long and hard and I realise that it is necessary or there is no advantage to getting rid of my husband other than not having to look at his miserable face again. But I must be sure that I will be OK financially etc.

S.'

Despite Collins's reassurances, this most recent email definitely looked as if she was cooling off. 'Luciano' swiftly sent off a reassuring reply.

'I think you will never worry about anything. We will take care of them and no one [will] point to you. That's guarantee[d]. This is our business. But sorry, we have to have the deposit before we proceed. That will be before Wednesday Aug 16. And why [would] you worry bout that? They don't have the time or days to check about the money, cause they will be gone. We are planning Aug 18 or 19 … and your husband Aug 20. We can arrange to meet you and get the key or we have our ways in without keys. And we have to have pic of the two guys and your husband too. If you don't have it we will figure out that.

Thanks.

Tony Luciano.'

It worked. Collins was back in a slightly more positive frame of mind.

'I'm back now.

I suppose you're right—I should just leave it to you and not worry—but I do worry.

I could send the keys of the apartment to you or leave them somewhere in Spain near the apartment for you to collect. There is a further complication about Spain though. He has a boat and could arrange to be away on it at any time. It's impossible for me to say where he will be until much closer to the time. In any case, I suppose we could stay in touch by text if he and I are on the boat. But if I'm on the boat I wouldn't want anything to happen to him there. I guess if he were to get news about his sons he would immediately return to the apartment to pack anyway.

I definitely have photos of my husband and I think I have one of the guys but I will have to look tomorrow and email them to you.

I know you say not to worry about the cash and that they won't have time to find out, but I have to consider what would happen if you couldn't get near the guys here in Ireland next weekend. And if I was to transfer the money to you on or before Wed, they could notice on Thursday or Fri before you've had a chance to get to them. This is a major concern for me. I can't get them suspicious of me in any way. I'm already walking a very fine line here, believe me. If it would do you, I think I could get approximately €13,000 without too many problems before Wednesday (not money that would be missed). How would it be if I sent that and paid a little more than the quoted fee after the job is done? I'm not sure how much cash there is in Spain but I think it is a considerable amount and would go a long way towards paying the total fee. Once my husband is taken care of, I'd be 'bringing him home' and any balance can be sent immediately, once I'm back here (a matter of days) Whatcha think?

If this is totally unacceptable to you, please confirm that you will be willing to do this job at a later date when I've had a chance to get the money together.

Kind regards.

S.'

'Luciano' wasn't about to let this one get away. Within the hour he wrote back, determined to broker the deal.

'Here's the deal. You can send $15,000 by Wed and after we arrive we can have the $30,000 which is the balance of the deposit. It will be the 18 of August … and the rest of the money, which is $45,000 no later than 72 hours after the job done. This is our contract or you will be our target. Sorry to say that but this is our policy. Now we need the pics, names and address for all of them.

One thing I want to tell you. Don't think what people think what you thinking. Think they know nothing and I guess you are not gonna worry. Let us do out job and just relax—cause if you worry you make a mistake and we both gonna be in trouble. Is that a deal?'

In Nevada there was bated breath as 'Luciano' waited to see if this stage of the plan would result in a nice large pay cheque. Collins kept them waiting but when she did reply, the one-time business woman was not about to seal the deal without haggling. As the deal progressed she slipped into business mode. Her language became that of a woman used to getting things done.

'Sorry for taking so long getting back to you.

Tony, I'm not trying to be difficult about the money. If you can get me out of the unbearable situation that I'm in and I don't get into trouble for, then it's money well spent as far as I'm concerned. What you suggested in your last email is very fair, but as I said before, I'm going to Spain on Wednesday and I'd have to take the cash and leave it somewhere for you. But if I do the sons could notice it gone after I leave and tell him my husband. Then the shit would hit the fan for me. I know you'd be taking care of him on Sunday but I'm afraid he would say it to someone. He's got close friends with him in Spain (in the apartment next door)—he might tell them.

I have to tell you I have absolutely no intention of being your next target by not paying the balance of any money I owe you after the jobs are done. You most definitely will be paid within 72 hours. I've got children of my own and intend on being around for them. That's another reason why I want to be as careful as possible that I don't end up in jail. I want to be absolutely sure that when I start this thing by paying you the booking deposit I'll be in a position to finish it by paying you what I owe. In addition there may possibly be one more person I might add to the list a little later, but I'll get this job done first.

I've been thinking about it all earlier today and I wonder if you wouldn't mind giving me some advice. Tell me honestly—would it look more 'believable' if one of the sons were to go first, followed a few months later by the other and then immediately by the father (as planned this time). The reason why I wanted to get it all done together was I thought I could take all the money to pay afterwards and no one would be around to notice, but maybe it's the wrong way. I know it would be a more expensive way to do it but please let me know if it would be better. What I'm thinking is, maybe I could borrow the $50,000 to pay for the others. I'm not very brave am I? But then again, you do this all the time—I've never in my life considered anything like this.

Another thing I need advice on is this. I used the computer at work (we all work together) to surf the net for a hitman. If the cops seize the computer could they find evidence of my search?

As this is the weekend, I won't be able to talk to the bank about a loan until Monday, so there's no way I can confirm if this thing will be on for next weekend until the bank sanctions a loan, but I will keep you informed all the way of my progress.

I'm hoping I will be able to talk to you later, but in the meantime, would you email me back and let me know what you think about the above.'

'Luciano' kept playing the game but was now trying to move things forward.

'First I don't know you[r] name. My plan is we will get close to you[r] two step son[s]. We can do that. This is our arrange … after we finish I will fly to Spain by myself like I said before, if you arrange to give me the key or not I will be in his apartment, and I will take him out to his boat and we will do it there. So that not gonna be any miss. But I have to pay the guys in Ireland to do their job. That's why I have to have some money by Wed. So … Monday have to get 15,000 euro and send it by FedEx for next day delivery. So it will be here by Wed —or you can go to other bank and transfer the money. Without that, sorry we can't do it. I know you will pay us later that's why we give you a break for the deposit. We trust you for that. But this people have to get pay [sic] too before the job. Put yourself in my shoes too.

You understand what I said, just calm down and let people think what you think. Be yourself and don't ever, ever worry about anything. Just tell your step [sons] I need the money for your girlfriend just for a week or any reason and tell them don't tell anyone about it. Or give them any reason and the money will be back in your bank.

Let me know ASAP. If I will send this people or not, also about the pic. We have to have ASAP too.

Thanks Baby.

Tony Luciano.'

Maybe it was the mention of the word 'baby' but Collins found time to talk. After all, this was an important transaction. But there was something else. The two were now beginning to flirt. Afterwards 'Luciano' wrote again. For him it was the middle of the afternoon on Saturday, 12 August.

'That's what I said we need 15,000 by wed and I will get the rest after the two son is gone. And about you[r] husband. I change my plan to his app, just let him jump. It depend about [sic] when. This is after we talk together over there. Let me know more info when he get[s] the news. I want do it the same day when he get[s] the bad news.

So 15,000 by wed and 30,000 by sun the 20 Aug and the rest after the husband. You still didn't get me the pic—I have to have it. We don't want to get wrong people and the last thin[g] what's your name?

Thanks,

Tony.'

Minutes later Collins was back. By now she was really into her character and was concerned not to miss anything out. For the moment she was thinking of the problems and the nerves had disappeared.

'Gee you got back to me fast—thanks!

Let me get this straight. Are you saying that if I FedEx €15,000 to you on Monday, to pay the people in Ireland, that you will do the rest and wait for the balance till after my husband is done? This is possible for me. But maybe I misunderstand. Please confirm.

You didn't say whether you think it is the best way to do it, all of them like this or one first and the other two later.

About the boat—I must explain. The boat is not in close proximity to the apartment and when you leave the apartment block there are lots of shops and vendors all around. They are open until very late and they know him well. I think it would be difficult to get him out without raising suspicion and remember, I need it to look like he has committed suicide after hearing about his sons. Also the boat is quite big and perhaps difficult for you to handle if you are on your own. I think it is important that I tell you exactly the way it is there. And also point out any complications that might arise. OK?

The apartment is on the top floor of a 14 storey apartment block. It has a private terrace and plunge pool on the roof. An Irish couple with whom he is very friendly own the apartment next door. They are in Spain now too, but I think they have tenants in it for the summer. I'm not sure, but I can find out later.

This couple also have a boat there, near his boat and if they are not in their apartment they will be living aboard their boat—another reason why you might find it difficult to get away with taking him out on it.

My husband is planning to go on a boat trip for a few days when I get there, but I don't know when this is or where. I really don't know that until we are going. But I think, wherever it is, when he gets a phonecall about his sons, he will immediately return to his apartment to pack to come home. Unless he decides to go directly to the airport from the marina. If he does this then I don't know how you would get him.

I will be there, as you know. How do you suggest we stay in touch so I'm not there when you get there? Also I will need to let you know when he gets the news about his sons and what he is doing then.

My husband has a bad heart—maybe when he gets the news about his sons you won't need to do anything at all (except get your money!) But I feel I should point out all the pit falls to you beforehand. Another complication could be his friends—they might come back to the apartment with us to sympathise with him. The Irish are like that! And there are lots of Irish friends of his out there.

In your experience, when you show up to 'take care of' someone, do they ask you who sent you?

Do they offer to pay you to kill that person instead of them? Just wondering.

S.'

'Luciano' had thought of something else, an answer to an earlier question.

'About the computer. Don't ever use the work computer. You have to delete every thing. Thanks.'

Collins had already thought of this. She was now using the laptop Howard had bought to do the accounts, when Downes & Howard didn't have a proper base. He'd forgotten it was in the house since her son Gary had taken it away to college with him. It had been knocking around for some time though.

'Yeah I'm worried about that. I was told by a guy in the computer company that services our computers that even if you delete stuff, it can be still accessed …

I'd have to take the computer from the office before I go. I better think of an excuse to do that.

I'm just wondering now if it might not be easier to wait until we return from Spain to do my husband. After all, you plan to do his sons on Sat 19th. Right? He'll get a call about it immediately and go home as soon as he gets a flight. Even if you hit him on Mon 21st I still have time to pay you don't I?

It's just an idea. The only thing is, one of my sons lives here with us and will be here, as will I.

Not sure how that would work. Again Tony, it must look like suicide for him. Or natural causes. This is vital. And the body can't disappear. It must be there.

S.'

Then she was back.

'OK, so do you intend for us to talk on the phone in Spain or to meet face to face? The money; am I to give it to you in cash? It's all going to happen within a few hours right? As far as I know, my husband has enough cash there for me to give you the equivalent of $30,000 in Euro. I'll be able to check how much cash he has when I get there on Wed and let you know. I won't be able to take it while he is there, but if you are going to be in the apartment, I can give you the combination to the safe and you can help yourself. Is that OK? He always likes to have a lot of cash with him, so I'm not sure if he would take the cash from the apartment while we are gone and you can check the money to satisfy yourself that it is there. But I would ask you not to touch it until he is gone. We can talk about it anyway. With everything going on he will be upset, therefore, I don't see a problem. I could FedEx the keys of the apartment with $15,000 on Monday.

Do you have any idea how long it would take for the authorities to release his body from Spain? I'll need to get home ASAP after you've done your bit to send the rest of the money to you. Will I have to stay there until they release the body or do you think I could leave, without causing too much suspicion and let them forward the body to Ireland afterwards? Perhaps you would know how this works?

Photos, I don't have a scanner here to send the photos. I'll have to source one tomorrow and send them to you then.

My name. Tony, if you knew me—I wouldn't harm a fly—seriously. I've just been put in such an impossible situation that I feel I really have to take drastic action. There's no point in going into the details of it with you, unless you need to know. Anyway, I want to sleep on it tonight and decide once and for all if I will be able to live with myself afterwards. I'm a real softy and there was a time when I really loved my husband, but he has truly killed that. But even though I can't stand him now and have been wishing him dead for a long, long time, I found it really upsetting when I read your emails and saw it there in black and white. The reality is fairly startling, especially for an un-violent person like me. I know he has asked for it and would do the same himself if he was in my position, but that doesn't make it easy for me.

I will let you know tomorrow for sure and will give you my name then—if I must! My son is around at the moment so I won't be able to talk on the phone tonight as I had hoped—but we will have to talk tomorrow. Is that OK?'

'Luciano' was now playing along as much as she was. He was close to earning a substantial sum of money. More than anything, he needed the deposit to be sent if the plan was to progress any further.

'Hello.

I want tell you that we are professional people here. We don't give a chance to anyone to make a deal with us, especially the target. Even if they offer us 10 mill euro we honor our contract. So don't ever worry about that.

So I want you [on] Monday [to] send the key, the pic and the money plus the combination of the safe and the address for all of them. If you have the address for the two guys which is the party, add that [it would] be great. Also I want to ask you if your husband have [sic] a gun or maybe we can use to kill himself or if not we let him jump from the 14th floor. I want you to stay with him till you leave Spain with his body. Don't leave him—it will be suspicious. That we recommend.

I need your phone number in Spain too. We can contact you there after we done in Ireland. We don't call each other by phone maybe is dangerous. Just email us and we reply fast.

Thanks.

Tony Luciano.'

Collins replied during lunch time on Sunday. The plan seemed to be coming together.

'To: Tony Luciano

Yes I can send you everything including the addresses.

My husband does not have a gun in Spain, so jumping seems like the only option. I'm wondering how you'd make him jump. By the way, it's a hotel / apartment complex. A lot of other apartments and hotel rooms have a view of it. There's a swimming pool on a roof of a six or seven storey building in the complex just below our apartment block. There are always lots of people sunbathing beside that pool. Thought you should know. When I talk to you I'll explain more.

About staying in Spain with my husband's body. Yes I agree that it would be the right thing to do. But in that case will you understand that I may not be back in Ireland within the 72 hour deadline to send you the rest of the money. That money will be in Ireland and I won't be able to touch it until I get back. As soon as I am there I'll send it to you.

Contacting each other while in Spain; I won't have access to internet while on the boat. How would I let you know when he's heard the news about the son?

Poisoning the sons—you still haven't explained. Perhaps you want to talk on the phone about it instead.

Tony, I still haven't made up my mind that I'm ready to go ahead with this just now. As I've told you—there's no doubt that we will be doing business, but not sure it will be this week.

One more thing, I have to be honest, part of me feels that this is a scam and that I will send the 15k euro and that will be the end of it or, even worse, that information will be given to the cops and I'll find myself behind bars.

As I said, I hope to talk to you today. I will email you when I'm on my own later or maybe you could email a number where I can reach you when I can. That would suit me better, if you don't mind. I have visitors today—which isn't ideal. It's not giving me much time to think.

S.C.'

So Collins was finally showing some sense and developing a sneaking suspicion that receiving badly written emails from a total stranger who contacts you from a website might not be 100% trustworthy. But her new found good sense didn't last long and she was soon back with more questions.

'The telephone number is the one I gave before. I'll email you when I can talk. Is that OK?

I've been trying to think of an excuse for removing the computer from the office. It's my husband's business and his sons work there too. I think it would be a good idea not to leave it there in case anyone decides to check it out.

I also have been thinking about getting the cashiers cheque. Here in Ireland, any time you buy a bank draft or cashier's cheque, the bank keeps a record of who you are and you have to do it at your own bank. It's regulation. Anyway, if there is any question of it at a later date I can say that I got it from my husband—that he told me to. And if I'm asked what he wanted it for, I can say he didn't appreciate being asked questions. He always told me not to question him, just do what I was told (which is true, actually).

In addition, if there's a FedEx record of the envelope—again I will say that I was asked at work to send it. I don't know what it was. What do you think?

Might never come to that anyway. Hopefully not anyway.'

Collins's concerns were of no interest to 'Luciano'. He wanted his money. Several hours later he started pushing for a phone call.

'Let me know when we can talk. We have no time. It will happen this weekend which is six days left. Just send FedEx through your company like you said and the cashier check. Don't write any name, we will do that in our secret account. But we will give the address that you can FedEx it to. You have to … I mean you have to trust us and the job will be done. Don't worry or panic and act normal—like nothing happen.

Thanks.

Tony.'

Collins got straight back to him. She began a rapid back and forth of emails as they discussed how to find the time to talk.

'OK then, I'm 90% decided to go ahead with it. I know you want me to leave it to you and not question you but I can't help it.'

'No that's the best way we can do it. We used our own staff to do it so. There push him out one time so there is no fingerprint or any evidences.'

'I'm still caught here with my sister and her husband. I was hoping that you could ring me tonight but I don't want them to see me checking emails and I don't want to seem impatient with them. As you said, I want to act normal. Can you email me your telephone number and I will ring you when I can?'

It was some time before 'Luciano' replied, for the first time allowing domesticity to intrude on the mafia persona.

'Sorry, I had something to do with my daughter. Just get back. My phone is 5868830198. You can call me any time Sharon.'

Collins replied later on the Sunday evening with yet more details.

'If you're going to Spain, you will have to fly to Malaga. I forgot to tell you that. Anyway I was just talking to my husband. The couple with the apartment next door to ours will not be in their apartment. They will either be on their own boat or gone home to Ireland. I'll know when I get there on Wed night.

My husband plans for us to take a boat trip to Puerto Banus on Friday and stay there until Sunday or Monday. In any case he will surely have to return to his apartment after he gets the "sad" news of his sons!

I will be able to give you my Spanish mobile number and if you get yourself a Spanish phone when you get there you will be able to text me and then I'd be able to tell you what we are doing. I probably wouldn't have access to internet most of the time.'

It appears that Collins wanted to call but just couldn't get away so she emailed 'Luciano' again.

'I'm still not in a position to talk on the phone but hopefully in a while. I have visitors staying in the house and I need total privacy to talk.

I'm assuming your people will put that substance in the guys' drink, is that it? Tony, as I said before, nearly every weekend those guys go to Kilkee, on the west coast of County Clare. They spend a lot of time in a bar there and they also go boating. But there is absolutely no guarantee that they will be there next weekend. Occasionally they go to visit cousins of theirs at the other side of the country. I can't think of the name of the place right now but it'll come to me. The country is small, so no matter where they are, it's only a few hours away. I assume this will not be a problem? I will do my best this week to find out what they intend doing and will

email you as soon as I can so your people can make
alternative hotel reservations.

Do you still intend travelling to Spain yourself?
It's quite a distance for you to have to travel. I don't
think there are any direct flights between the US
and Malaga.'

At this stage she was discussing details as if planning to
hook up with a couple of friends. She kept forgetting what
was at stake but 'Luciano' kept reeling her in … the deal
would have to be closed fast.

'I was in Malaga before and I know how to get
there. From Madrid or Barcelona I'm planning on
it so don't worry about that for now. I'm so excited
to talk to you on the phone.
Tony Luciano.'

As Collins played the perfect hostess 'Luciano' began to
get impatient. He tried to phone her. No reply. It was
Monday in Las Vegas now. 'Luciano' emailed again.

'I'm sorry to call you wrong time but time is running
out. We have to know where we at. So I'm going to
do some business and I will be back.
Waiting for your call …
Thanks. Tony.'

Collins finally got a bit of privacy and they were able to
talk. After the call 'Luciano' sent another email … just to
make absolutely sure he had made his point clear.

Every morning, Sharon Collins would arrive at court, clutching this neat black folder. As the day progressed she would write a steady stream of notes on yellow Post-It pads. (*Courtpix*)

Essam Eid leaves the Central Criminal Court after being sentenced to six years for extortion and two counts of handling stolen property.
(*Courtpix*)

HIT MAN FOR
IRE

'THE PERFECT SOLUTION'

ME
W TO ORDER
CURE EMAIL
PLOYMENT

Hitman is the perfect solution for your killing needs. We offer a variety of professional assassination services available worldwide. Whether you are trying to put an end to a domestic dispute or eliminate your business competitors, we have the solution for you.

We are a privately-owned independent enterprise that specializes in reliable contract killings.

We take our business very seriously and are the best at what we do.

Assassinations are the most practical solutions to common problems. Thanks to the Internet, ordering a hit has never been easier. We manage a network of freelance assassins, available to kill at a moment's notice. All you have to do is send us an email, along with the details, and wait for further instructions. All the correspondence is done through our secure online forms

We offer several options to suit the specific needs of our clients.

Each case is analyzed and designed for maximum protection and satisfaction.

Basic contracts start at base cost plus expenses. We require a photograph, bio, and address of the target, along with a deposit. The balance is due no later than 72 hours after the job is done.

Home | Order | Secure Email | Employment
Copyright 2006 Hit man for Hire. All Rights Reserved.

The homepage of www.hitmanforhire.net, seen here for the first time, on which Essam Eid advertised his services as a hitman.

His defence claimed that the site had nothing to do with him.

Sharon Collins's partner, P.J. Howard, leaves the court after delivering his victim impact statement on the day of her sentencing. Despite his plea to the judge not to impose a custodial sentence, Collins was sentenced to six years in jail.

Niall Howard (left) and Robert Howard (right) arrive at the
Central Criminal Court during the third week of Collins
and Eid's trial. (*Courtpix*)

Sharon Collins was flanked throughout the trial by her sons Gary (left) and David (right).

(Courtpix)

Engle told FBI Agent Ingrid Sotelo (above) that she and Eid had made ricin at their home in Vegas, which they then brought to Ireland.

Ricin comes from the castor bean (right); the same nondescript small brown bean that produces castor oil.

Teresa Engle (above) tried to extort €100,000 from Robert Howard along with Eid, but she told the gardaí that she was simply another victim; she was merely Eid's pawn, an unwilling partner in all the subterfuge. She agreed to testify against Eid at his trial.

(*Press 22*)

Collins moved into P.J. Howard's luxurious home with her sons in 1998, shortly after meeting him. He said in court that he would have no difficulty moving in to live with her again.

(*Courtpix*)

Radio host Gerry Ryan and his producer, Siobhán Hough, were called as witnesses during the trial. Collins had sent emails to his show alleging P.J. Howard had strange and kinky sexual preferences. These allegations were refuted by Howard.

Essam Eid worked in the Bellagio in Las Vegas as a poker dealer. He claimed he earned close to $100,000 a year in tips at the casino.

Private Brian Buckley, who gave evidence in the trial, was unwittingly drawn into the affair after he happened upon hitmanforhire.net.

(*Courtpix*)

EMPLOYMENT

Name			
Phone			
Best Time to Contact			
E-mail			
Location City/Country			
Experience:			
Criminal Record:			
Special Skills: Firearms Explosives Poisons Martial Arts Torture			
Employment Objective:			
Encrypted Message:			
	submit reset		
	THIS EMAIL IS ENCRYPTED AND SECURE		
	Hit the "submit" button only once. It may take a couple of seconds to register, but it will go through		

...ins came across hitmanforhire.net she initially filled
...loyment form, to try to gauge whether this site was
...ing what it said, or if it was a comedy site, as so many
...e. In a prophetic flash she put down 'none yet' beside
...Record'.
...he didn't receive an automated response, she then
...e 'Secure Email' form using lyingeyes98@yahoo.ie as
...email address.

(Courtpix)

Sharon Collins is led away after being found guilty of conspiring to kill P.J. Howard and his sons.

Eugene O'Kelly (left) issued a statement to the media on Sharon Collins's behalf after she was sentenced to six years in prison. Standing from left to right. Eugene O'Kelly, Collins's son David, her former husband Noel and her eldest son Gary.

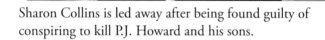
(Sasko Lazarov/Photocall Ireland)

'If you can't send the money today forget about it. It will be too late. My people not wait. Plus I will pay them the rest from my pocket till you pay me after the job done. Now it's up to you. Sorry but I have to give them the green light and I can't if no money. Sorry the pressure on me. By the way you have nice voice. Sorry to say that.'

Once 14 August dawned in Ireland Collins was back at her desk in Downes & Howard. She had made up her mind. Secure in the supposed knowledge that she was using an anonymous email she was all business that summer morning.

'I will be sending the money later today. It's 11 a.m. here now so once I get the envelope to FedEx by 5 p.m. today we're OK. Will you email the address for delivery? I'm at work right now—have to behave as normal and when I'm sent to the bank later I will sort out the money. Don't worry, I'm going to do it, I've decided.

I also need to spend some time here with one of the sons to find out what he will be doing next weekend. Will let you know as soon as I do.

Thanks for your phone number—will you email me the correct prefix.

Talk later, Sharon'

The address was quickly forthcoming. The Camden Cove Street conmen lost no time sending Teresa Engle's name with the address in North Las Vegas. The bank details given were with the local branch of the Bank of America and in the name of Essam Eid.

'Just let me know either way so I want know what we are looking for. I will talk to you later, Sweetie.'

Collins had come to a decision.

'I've decided to parcel up the money and send it that way. I will probably put something else in with it to make it look like a present. I'll also put in the photos and the keys. I'll email you the address, combination and directions etc.

Just busy at work right now and under pressure to get everything done so I can get away early to send off the parcel.

Will email you later and let you know tracking number etc.'

Finally! 'Luciano' was delighted.

'OK. Just be careful. Talk to you later then.'

CHAPTER 8:

TONY AND SHARON

That afternoon Collins went to her local bank and withdrew €13,000. She made up the balance with her credit card. She was ready to go. But she would not have the chance to send the money until the following day. And she had to select something suitable to put in the package. Later that evening she emailed hire_hitman@yahoo.com. While gardaí would eventually find she had talked to phones registered to Essam Eid over 70 times, during these few days in mid August it was proving very difficult for her to organise the murders.

'Tony,

I told you that you could ring me but my son came home unexpectedly—wants to spend some quality time with me this evening as I'm going away on Wednesday so I put the cell phone away and put it on silent.

When he goes to bed later tonight, I'll let you know.

Sharon.'

Later that night she found time to talk. Collins may have been in work that day but over her lunch hour and again after work she called 'Luciano' from her desk. After the call 'Luciano' was feeling decidedly flirtatious. Whether this was just him showing his way with the ladies or because Collins had turned on the charm again; Eid was flirting openly with her, albeit by email.

> 'I guess from your voice no one can touch you and I guess you are beautiful too. Sorry to say that. There is no way to me or any one killing you. I hope we received by Thursday and go there. I will call the guys even if I pay them from my pocket. We are still on. Just act normal we gonna be OK. I'm leaving Friday from here to be in Spain by Saturday afternoon. I will text msg you and let you know that I'm there. I will try to email you my pic too but don't make fun of me … lol.'

Whatever the conversation had been, it had suddenly changed 'Luciano' from a tough talking mafioso type to a bashful school boy right down to the text speak. Whatever had been said, 'Luciano' for one certainly wanted a little more conversation.

> 'I tried to call you but no answer. I will try again later on. I did send my pic to you and I have my daughter in one of them. I have no idea why.
> Tony.'

Eventually Collins responded to him. It was apparent that she had also fallen into a more coquettish mood and once again the words kept flowing.

'Finally I have a chance to email with no one breathing down my neck.

Again I must apologise for not being able to take your calls tonight. I though I'd be on my own but my son, who's 20, came home much earlier than I expected. He's a good kid and said he wanted to spend some quality time with me as I'm going away on Wednesday. We were watching a movie and chatting and, at the time, I was trying to email you, but as I said, we are always, always having problems with internet connections at the house, so I lost the very long email that I had hoped to send you.

Anyway, what I was saying was—thank you for the photos. Your daughter is beautiful and clearly loves her dad and you're very handsome yourself. Italian of course!

I had to smile when I saw your photos. For as long as I can remember I've been saying that I would love a sexy yellow sports car—and I've always wanted to visit Las Vegas. Maybe you'll take me for a ride in yours if I ever get there! Now that's cheeky isn't it?!

Anyway, I was sitting with my son last night and thinking—if he only knew what his mother was planning. He definitely would wonder if he ever knew me at all. My boys would be devastated if they thought I would do such a thing. My other son is nearly 23 and works in Dublin. I miss him a lot.

We are very close. In fact my boys are everything to me. I got married (for the first time) when I was 19. It was a disaster. There was no divorce in Ireland at the time, but I got an annulment from the Church and when divorce was introduced I got one. I didn't have to resort to extreme measures at the time. I can get on quite well with my ex-husband now. I think it's important for children that parents try to get along, even when the relationship breaks down. Otherwise the children question their own worth.

I suppose you think I want to be rid of my husband so I can get what he has? Well I do want to inherit—I want my home and an income, of course I do. But there's a lot more to it than that. For one thing, he resents any time I spend with my boys and tried to keep me away from them. That's a reason why my son wanted to take advantage of being with me last night while my husband's in Spain. My husband wants to control every moment of my life and has a dreadful temper. And he makes sure I have no money of my own. But the main reason I'm doing this is because he is continually trying to force me to go out and pick up a stranger for sex. He finds the idea of it exciting and insists I must do it or I'm out and he will make sure that I have absolutely nothing. Well I will not do that. No way! The mother of my boys is not a slut. I think it's disgusting that a man would want his woman to be with another man. He never, ever stops pushing for it. Frankly I don't care what he does. I don't mind if he has sex with hookers or transvestites (of which he is particularly fond) everyday but leave me out of it. He has gone so far that I'm at the stage now when I would be happy if I never had to hear of sex again. I would be perfectly content on my own now with no man. I certainly will never marry or live with someone again.

You might ask yourself why I don't just leave and sue him but it wouldn't work believe me. I'm in a very vulnerable situation. And because of the way he has things tied up I'm afraid his boys are going to suffer now—and I really regret that. I wish so much that it didn't have to be like this, but then again, I know that if my husband was dead and they were still here they'd screw me anyway. In fact I'm sure of it. So now I want to protect myself and my boys.

Gee Tony I must be boring you out of your mind. It's the last thing you need to know. Sorry—I do go on.

To get back to business. I still haven't found out where the guys will be this weekend. They probably don't know themselves yet. More than likely though, it will be Kilkee.'

'Luciano' probably didn't give much thought to Collins's allegations about Howard. It is likely that she made them up, simply to give herself and excuse for her own actions. Howard's sons had also been nothing but kind to her. She most likely invented the allegations to ease her own conscience. Either way, 'Luciano' probably didn't care one way or another as everything was going to plan. Collins's flirtatious emails also made it more interesting.

'Thanks for your comment. I bet you look so beautiful too. Maybe after we done the business— maybe it will be my pleasure to have dinner with you. You gonna pay for it???? Hahaha.'

Collins had finally found suitable photos to send on the computer at work. There was a nice one of her and Howard from the Christmas party, which she emailed immediately.

'Tony,
    As I said, I'm not sure which photos were which while I was sending them. You'll be able to tell which one is my husband … and I'm the devil in the red dress!
    The photo with the guy on the left is the younger one and the one on the right the older.
    I'm with them now, so email later.
    Sharon.'

'Luciano' didn't take long to get back to her, though his tone was more serious, not having yet had confirmation that the money had actually been sent.

'Hello Sharon,
    You look so great I can't wait to see you. OK let's talk business. We agreed before 50% down which is 45,000 and we went down to 15,000 and you tell me after all done…sorry Sharon we don't know each other yet to do that and I'm sorry.
    I did trust you for the 30,000 and now I feel you take advantage—that's what I feel. So if I didn't

receive the money or some of them (15,000) by Thur forget about it well! Email me the tracking number or let me know wither one or what you gonna do.
Thanks.'

Collins didn't get back to him immediately as she was busy covering her tracks in Ennis. When she finished in work she copied the important files she needed from the computer onto a disc so they would be saved when the computer disappeared according to her plan. After all, even if she was successful, the business would still have to keep running. But his last email worried her a bit. She began to think twice about what she was about to do. At one point she started to write an abrupt email to him.

'Just one thing Tony. There is a disclaimer at the bottom of your website which states that the website is a parody. Please comment.'

The disclaimer was a copy of the one on the hitman.us website, a convenient way for hitmanforhire.net to cover itself if people did get suspicious. It had been displayed at the bottom of the website since Collins had first visited it two weeks previously. But she decided she didn't want to irritate 'Luciano'. Not while there was still business to be done. It was for this reason that she typed another email.

'OK Tony I promise I wasn't trying to take advantage—honest. But I wouldn't blame you for thinking I was. I'm just nervous. I haven't been very happy with my parcel and I'm worried someone will examine it. I am going to try to figure out a better way of concealing the cash in the parcel before I drop it off later.

'OK friends again. There is something else you might be able to help me with though. I had hoped to take the computer out of the offices this evening and say I was bringing it to our computer maintenance firm. Anyway when I said it, one of the sons told me that the technician who does out work is on holiday and told me to leave it in the office and they would bring it over themselves. Now I can't think of an excuse to remove it tonight or tomorrow. They know I have a laptop at home and won't need it there. So is there anyway that any of you doing the job here could let themselves into the office and remove the computer after they have finished the job. I could arrange to leave keys somewhere for them to collect? I feel that the computer is the one thing that could point the finger at me (apart from the cash being discovered in the parcel.) Is it possible—you did say that the guy who will be working is German right? There's a guy …
Sharon.'

Collins never sent the email and ended up deleting it. She fiddled around with the parcel until she was happy with it. €15,000 in cash isn't that easy to wrap discreetly. But she eventually mustered up the courage to send it.

When she left the office she headed to Shannon Airport with a neat parcel containing €15,000 in cash, and, so it didn't look suspicious, a pair of goggles she had found in a cupboard at home. They were supposed to be for some kind of computer game, not something she'd miss. They'd do. She made it to the FedEx office before they closed and filled out the docket in the name of an Anthony Howard, addressing it to Teresa Engle at the Camden Cove Street address. Back at home she tried to email 'Luciano' again after unsuccessfully trying to ring.

'Now I know for sure you sleep as I've just been ringing you. Well I'm glad—I'll need you at your best …

What I really need to know urgently is where to leave the keys of the office for your people and what name to put on the envelope.

I will not put the address in the envelope with the keys—I will give it out to you after you receive the money and confirm that the job is still on. But I will give you some details for getting into the office.

If they leave it until late there will be no one around (there is a cleaner who comes on her own time, but not at night.)

There is an alarm so they must do the following— two locks on the outside door. It's not a very secure door anyway. Light switch to the right of the door. Straight up the stairs and into the reception.

Sometimes the door at the top of the stairs is locked but the key is always in the door lock. Light switch to the left of the reception door just inside reception area. Walk behind reception. There are two doors behind the desk and also an opening to a small area behind the desk. The alarm is just inside this opening on the wall. The code is [number given]. This turns the alarm on and off. The computer that I am concerned about is the one at the reception desk. No need to take the monitor or keyboard etc just the hardware left on the floor under the desk.

It would be a good idea if the alarm was turned on again when they leave, same code. And leave the door locked as before.

There's a safe in the office but there is never much money in it. Just a few hundred euro. I don't want it touched. I just want it to look like one of the sons took the computer themselves for repair or something.

I've just saved everything important for work on a CD and have it with me. If I don't hear from you in time I will decide myself where to leave the key and let you know.

There is something else I want done – I want an email sent to my husband's email address. I will give you the details tomorrow. No time now. Trying to get ready for trip.

Sharon.'

'Luciano' tried to ring her back but was unsuccessful.

'I guess we have a problem to talk on the phone. I just wondering is all info in the package … what's there beside the money? Is everything we need inside?

> Don't get mad when I see you in Malaga if I like you I will kiss you … if I don't you do it. I just joke.
> Thanks.
> Tony.'

It was at this point he suddenly realised Collins was not going to be contactable for the next few days.

> 'You gonna have you laptop with you in Spain? In case I want to contact you?'

Still no answer. Collins was having difficulties with the dial up. 'Luciano' tried again, not telling the entire truth.

> 'Everything is done. I did send my people to Ireland and I send them the deposit that they need and I'm getting ready to Malaga. Is any more info you can give me? I will try to call you again. Maybe I get through this time or try to call me back.
> Tony.'

Collins finally got the internet working again.

> 'Oh by the way Tony, I know you were ringing me earlier but I wasn't in a position to talk at the time. Funny, now I've managed to send several short emails but before that when I was trying to send a long message, I lost it every time—four times to be exact.
> Now I don't know what I've said and what I've left out. I would be able to talk on the phone at

approximately 1.30 a.m. my time if we can't get everything sorted by email before we meet in Spain. Did you get my message from earlier today regarding someone who works in security here? Is there any chance he could have any connection to your people in Ireland?

Am I driving you mad with questions and suggestions? OK I'll wait until I hear from you before emailing again. Sharon.'

'Call me later on when you have a chance … or I will call you. Tony.'

'I can talk now or anytime for the next two or three hours. I realise it is just after midnight here now. So if you are in a position to talk, please ring.
Sharon.'

The conspirators managed a couple of brief phone calls that evening. Nothing much, no time for any serious flirting—a maximum of five minutes snatched by Collins during the evening. Collins was also keeping an eye on the FedEx parcel which was slowly making it's way to Las Vegas. It arrived the next morning. Eid was in the shower and Engle was at work so it was Lisa who signed for the delivery. That night 'Luciano' was back at the computer.

'Hello Baby,
I tried to reach you several times but no answer. I guess you are not like me. You sleep a lot and I'm not. You can call me any time, I'm always up.
Bye Baby.'

Collins had left for Spain and it was not until Thursday when she was settled that she managed to get away and write a longer email with the details of the job in hand. She named those she wanted killed.

'The people you want information about are as follows:

The family name is Howard. There is P.J. Howard (57) and his two sons Robert (27) and Niall (23). P.J. Howard spends most of his time in the Costa del Sol in Spain. He has an apartment in Fuengirola, approximately 20 minutes from Malaga Airport on the motorway. The address, [she gave him the exact address]. This is a hotel and apartment complex. The entrance to which is beside the bus station and then ask the taxi driver to continue straight on to Calle Jac into Benevente. There is an entrance between Coyote Dance (disco) and Karaoke Video Café (bar). There are a lot of shops in the entrance with their merchandise on display as you walk through. When you go past approx three shops turn left and the door to the apartment block is on the right. Any of the shop owners can direct you to Torre [number given].

P.J. Howard also has a boat in Benalmedena and spends most weekends there on the boat.

Robert Howard and Niall Howard live in Ballaghboy, Doora, Ennis, Co Clare. To reach their house, [she then gave precise details of how to find their house, as well as a visual description of it].

Niall drives a BMW (small one) and Robert drives a Land Rover. They also have a house in Kilkee on the west coast of Co Clare. The address is [names address], Kilkee. They usually go there at weekends and often have cousins and friends stay with them. There is a possibility that they might go to a seaside resort called Ballybunion in Co Kerry this weekend. Will find out and let you know.

The Howard's have a company called Downes & Howard Ltd. The office address is 7A Westgate Business Park, Kilrush Road, Ennis, Co. Clare. Driving from Ennis Town in the Kilrush direction go through the traffic lights at a shop called Coote. Go past Seat Car Sales on the left. Then turn right into Westgate Business Park—it's opposite another car dealer (not sure of the name). There is a sign for John O'Dwyer Hardware and other businesses in the Business Park. Then turn right. Various shop units are there on the left. Go as far as Aids to Independence which is the last shop in the first block and there is a gap. The door for Downes & Howard offices is to the side of Aid to Independence. It is not marked, no sign. Just a timber double door.

There is a house on the Clare Road (Limerick Road) in Ennis. Leaving Ennis town, heading in the Limerick direction there is a filling station and car sales called Estuary (Francie Daly is the proprietor and his name is on a sign). Immediately after this there is a turn right—don't take it. Immediately after that there is a blue house, then a yellow house with a Sale Agreed sign outside it. The seller is Era Leyden Auctioneers. No one lives in the house.

Behind the house beside the central heating boiler there is a concrete block and keys under it.

I will forward any further information that you need as soon as I have it.

Will ring you later.'

Over the next few days the two kept in touch by phone. Collins rang Eid numerous times between 17th and the 23rd of August. On the 23rd there was a flurry of contact as the final details were arranged. The deposit had arrived and the final touches were being put to the plan which would see Engle flying into Shannon a few days later. That morning Collins emailed 'Luciano' again.

'For guys I would say they will go to their usual place at the weekend—like I told you before. Usually they go on Friday afternoon or evening.

The hotel you mention is very close to the apartment but we may not be there. He plans to travel. Will know closer to the time.

I will try ringing you on that number it would be easier for me if we could talk.'

And talk they did—Collins called him a total of eleven times that day, the longest conversation lasting almost ten minutes. On the 25th they spoke again, Collins was determined to hammer out every last detail of the plot. The next day she was back at the keyboard. Whether Collins was panicking or trying to ensure that nothing would go wrong is unknown, but the emails suggest she was afraid of something going wrong. The Mexican marriage certificate was bothering her again.

'Hi Tony,

As I said to you last night—my husband must be first. If not, well there isn't much point at all in any of this and also I would have a lot of trouble getting my hands on the cash. The manner in which I got married would be questionable and I could find myself with absolutely nothing. I can't explain any further right now but believe me; the two boys must be first. So it will be back to the drawing board.

Are you sure your woman can't approach them in the bar as we discussed last night? I don't think it would be too hard to offer to buy them a drink and tell them that she knows their father.

It's believable—she met my husband in a night club in Spain. They were friendly for a while and he brought her boating and entertained her with drinks and meals out etc. She knows where he is from in Ireland and that he has a holiday home in Kilkee that his sons use most weekends. She sees the sons and thinks they must be his sons, as they look so much like him, especially the younger and smaller one. She would like to treat them to a drink and tells them to say hello to him for her when they next see him. They never get a chance to do that.

That would work, I think. She doesn't need to be with them for long as she can say she is with friends and must go. Then if you like, you could wait until we come home from Spain and see my husband then.

Just one other thing, do the guys have to be together? Could you do what you planned to one and maybe something else to the other?

I will try to ring you in a little while—but I know you don't always understand what I am saying and now my voice is going and it may be difficult to hear me. I've been having asthmatic attacks all week. I haven't suffered for years, but the stress of the situation is killing me. At this stage I feel like jumping from the apartment myself. Honestly I really need to get this done as soon as possible. I can't endure what it's doing to me. And I am terrified!

We are going back to the apartment tomorrow. Probably will be there around 9 p.m. but not sure what time yet. My son is meeting people he met so hopefully he won't be around.

Just one more thing—it will be obvious that someone deliberately wants the guys gone, won't it? Is there any way to avoid this? Maybe I am asking the impossible. If it's any good to you—they are probably in the bar right now.

And Tony, the computer in the office – it must go. That's vital. Just throw it in the sea or something.

Now about the money—to clarify:

What I was saying is that I always knew that I only had a total of 80k approximately to spend, including the 15k that I sent.

I propose paying it like this: Full Price $100,000 less amount paid 15,000 (we will say equal to dollars) = $85,000. Less money in safe 11,000 (again we will say equal to dollars.

Balance to pay afterward $74,000 US dollars. I will get the money changed into dollars somewhere before I pay you.

Does this clarify what I have? There just is not anymore cash there—unless I find some that I don't know about, and if I do it's yours. Are you satisfied with this? I sincerely hope so.

Talk to you soon,

Sharon.'

A few hours later she sent another email. Collins was now consumed by what she was doing. It took over her every thought. She wanted the murders to happen, so she could get on with her life. This is perhaps why she could not stop issuing instructions by email and snatched phone calls.

'You can get an Aer Lingus flight out of Cork Airport every morning at around 7 a.m. If you could get to the guys today or tonight you or your guy—or both of you—could be on tomorrow morning's flight and everything could be done by tomorrow. Too ambitious?

Talk soon,

Sharon.'

An hour later she rang him again before deciding it was better to put her thoughts in writing.

'To Tony,

Just a fast email—I will ring you later if possible. I wonder if you had the right house for the guys. It's a grey terraced house, [house number given] I think. There's a row of houses and it's the second last one on the right. Not a big fancy house, very ordinary.

About my husband—I really want it to look like suicide or natural causes. Will you think again about jumping from the window? I think that it would be a very believable thing for a man to do if he heard that his only two sons were dead—and it would be easy for you if there are two of you. You could be in his bedroom when he goes in, curtains closed and window open behind the curtains. Grab him by each arm and just throw him out very fast. Fourteen floors to fall should definitely do it. But if you have any better idea go ahead, just as long as it doesn't look like anyone else was involved. Also he would not be the kind of guy who would slash his wrists. Too much like a woman's thing to do!

Anyway will try to ring you later from the ladies restroom.
Sharon.'

But their plans were not going to go as smoothly as Collins had hoped. The so-called hitman she was placing all her hope in was not as smooth an operator as he made out.

CHAPTER 9:

FROM VEGAS TO ENNIS

The plot was in place—all that was needed now was some kind of action. Eid had booked the flight for Teresa Engle to fly to Shannon from Atlanta on 28 August. She would be staying in the Queen's Hotel in the centre of Ennis. Despite attempts to inveigle Private Buckley, who had no idea of the events that were unfolding, to come along for the ride after 'John Smith' too had faded into the background, Eid approached his friend Ashraf Gharbeiah to go along as the second person and booked him onto a flight a day after Engle. What was to happen in Ennis in the last days of August 2006 was either an abortive attempt to take this heist to the next level or the hapless criminals taking their preparation to levels that would make a method actor quake.

Whatever the reasoning behind it, Engle was on the plane that flew into Shannon on 29 August and booked into the Queens Hotel. Using the hotel as a base she started testing out the directions in Collins's emails. Collins was under the impression that the hit was about to take place after her flurry of emails from Spain but Engle did no more than look on this occasion, scoping and planning and fixing each location on the list. She would later insist in court, where she had been granted immunity from prosecution and was waiting to be sentenced for her part in the Royston sting, that her purpose in Ireland was to facilitate the real evil doer—Ashraf Gharbeiah who was due in the country to dispatch the Howard brothers. Gharbeiah on the other hand would tell a completely different story to the detectives who called him to get to the bottom of the Irish trip.

Whatever reason Engle travelled to Ireland, either a summer assassination or a simple recce mission for the con that was to come, she set off on that warm August evening along the broad, straight road out of town. Just as Collins had described she passed the shop called Coote and soon came to the car dealers. She walked past the shops and offices that made up the business park looking for Unit 7a. Downes & Howard was yet another anonymous building in the concrete expanse. She spent some time familiarising herself with the layout of the business park before heading back towards Ennis town.

Meanwhile in Spain, Collins was getting worried about whether or not things were going according to plan. She wrote to 'Luciano' again after another brief phone call.

> 'Hi Tony,
>   Thanks for getting back to me so quickly. I'll stop fretting about how to get the money to you. We'll figure that out when we get to it.'

The following day Gharbeiah flew to Ireland. He and Engle met up and this is where the narrative splits into two different accounts. Engle's version involved her meeting him at the Queens Hotel once he arrived. Once again, she went for a walk around the town but this time she had company. It was a pleasant, late summer evening as they walked the narrow streets. Engle brought him along the road out of the town centre to the business park where they reconnoitred the town. According to Engle, Gharbeiah had arrived in Ireland with a rattling bag of medicines that could be combined in particular ways to cause heart failure in an unsuspecting victim. He had access to a wide variety of drugs in his work as an emergency medical technician and certainly, the Foxglove compound Ouabain, which can be used to treat irregular heart beats and can have the opposite affect if mis-administered, had been discussed through hitmanforhire.net when 'John Smith' was still touting for work. Engle was adamant that harm was due to be done to the Howard brothers on this first visit but equally adamant that whatever the plan was she did not know anything about it. Her role in all of this was to be the scout she said. Yet there was an email from 'Luciano' on 28 August to Private Buckley, sent the day before she arrived in Ireland, asking for assistance.

'Hello Brian. Please help us out for this. I need some strong poison. One of us will be there at Shannon 7.20 coming from the States and we can't ship this stuff for security reasons, you know that. So please help us out. We will pay and I will owe you favourite. Thanks Brother.
Tony.'

According to Engle's story Gharbeiah intended to spike some wine or 'liquor' and accordingly they paid a visit to the local supermarket and stocked up. But they did not wait another day and take the trip to Kilkee for the weekend, where they had a fair idea from Collins's comprehensive emails where to find the two Howard brothers. Instead, according to Engle's version of events, Gharbeiah got cold feet and pulled out of the plan before heading back to the States the following day.

Gharbeiah, on the other hand, told a rather different story. He agreed that his old friend Eid approached him at the end of August and asked him to take a trip to Ireland to help Engle dispose of the Howard brothers. He said Eid was very confident of his latest squeeze's homicidal capabilities, and explained this was why he hadn't bothered going himself. He did, however, mention that the job was going to be very well paid. At the time Gharbeiah was going through a particularly messy divorce, so he decided to tag along. He insisted his motives were perfectly pure though. He simply wanted to persuade Engle not to carry out the killings. His friend bought the tickets and he found himself flying from Chicago to Shannon. Once he touched down he headed straight to Engle's hotel. They met in the bar of the Queen's Hotel.

Over the next hour and a half, he said he set to work persuading her to allow Robert and Niall Howard to continue living their lives. He described a very different creature to the mousey woman who gave evidence in court; the woman gardaí said was a shadow of herself when she was arrested in Ireland on her second visit. Gharbeiah described a loud, brash woman with the morals of an alley cat. He described that meeting in the bar of the Queen's

Hotel as having an eerie quality. He felt he was in the presence of someone who had no respect for human life. He found her vulgar and ethically 'not right'. He said he was reminded of the strange request from Eid earlier that year when Eid had said Engle wanted the unfortunate Todd Engle killed.

This latest development showed too much of a predilection for violence for his taste. She never told him how she planned to kill the Howard boys, he told the FBI, and she never showed him a weapon but he was satisfied she intended to carry out the job. She even nonchalantly mentioned the pay packet at the end of it. After an hour and a half Gharbeiah felt convinced that he had in fact managed to save the brothers' lives. He went and had dinner before returning to the bar where he stayed for the rest of the night. In Gharbeiah's account there are no trips to Westgate Business Park or liquor runs to the supermarket. The only two elements that coincide in both accounts are Gharbeiah's arrival and departure dates. As described by Engle he flew back to Chicago on 1 September while she stayed on. She had also been booked on a flight back to the States on the first day of September but she had more work to do in Ireland.

On Friday, 1 September, Collins emailed 'Luciano' again with the news that would send Engle on a whistle stop trip to Fuengirola.

'Hi Tony,

Very little time here. I will leave the keys at the hotel. I will pay your people myself because a friend of ours—an elderly man here—has given my husband money to mind for him and I want to keep it safe for him. He's a very good friend—you understand? I can meet them the following day or maybe after they have done it.

There is no landline in the apartment. We plan to stay on the boat tonight and I hope to bring my son with me so, in this way, no one will be at the apartment tonight and they can look around.

My husband would know a BB gun immediately —he is a gun dealer himself and very familiar. If I get the chance I will get one, but to get the chance will be difficult. They will be able to buy one with no difficulty in the shops in the Las Palmeras complex around the apartment block.

The guys told me that they are going to Kilkee, so hopefully everything will be ok there.

Talk soon.'

'Luciano' got back to her as soon as possible to update her and to convince her the job would be carried out.

'Hello Sharon. Here's the deal. Please don't call me a lot. We will call you when the job is done. We can't find the guys at all so we gonna do it at their office. Sorry it take more time than we thought but the job will be done, just relax. We will let you know as soon as we done it.

We change out reservation at the hotel in Malaga to El Puerto, Costa del Sol. I don't know how it is but we don't care. Other hotel we will stay at Clare Inn, Newmarket on Fergus, Dromoland in Ireland. I don't know how far from the office but we don't care either. Just let you know where we stay at.

After the job done like we agree that we gonna get pay. Max the 3rd Sept. I will let you know where and how. €11,000 and $47,000 USD. If we need info we will call you. Just relax yourself and let us do our job.

Thanks,

Tony'

More than anything, Collins wanted the conspiracy to conclude. She could not help but issue instruction after instruction. She quickly wrote back with more 'helpful' information.

'You can get an Aer Lingus flight out of Cork airport every morning at around 7 a.m. If you could get to the guys today or tonight you or your guy—or both of you—could be on tomorrow morning's flight and everything could be done by tomorrow.

Too ambitious?

Talk soon.

Sharon.'

So Engle went to Spain. She did not visit Kilkee before she left Clare. Her one encounter with P.J. Howard's sons would not take place until the end of September when the web of intrigue finally melted away. She took a Ryanair flight from Shannon Airport, unimpressed by the no frills approach calling it a 'small airline'.

When she arrived in Fuengirola the keys to Howard's penthouse apartment were waiting for her at the front desk of the hotel. The envelope they were in had her name on it. She took the keys but did not go up to the apartment. The hot sun was making her feel dizzy and there was always the risk that Collins hadn't managed to empty the apartment. The hotel complex was bright and noisy, the sky impossibly blue, and the street vendors loud and chattering. The scores of holiday makers who had come for an August of sun, sand and sangria were underfoot and beetroot red, thronging the beachfront and infesting the dun coloured sand leading down to the azure sea. Everywhere she looked there were British and Irish pubs. The stalls around the hotel complex sold a mixture of cheap Spanish tat and ridiculously over priced designer baubles. In some ways, it was a little like home.

She travelled out to the marina to try and find the boat even though the information she had from the hitmanforhire.net emails suggested that the boat would be rather full this evening but despite wandering around the port for a while she couldn't find Howard's boat. She checked in with Las Vegas and reported that the 'Heartbeat' could not be found. It was not proving to be a very productive trip. There was one last thing to check before heading back to Fuengirola. Collins had mentioned, in her many phone calls to Eid, that when she was on the boat it was possible to email from a nearby internet café. Engle verified its existence before she headed back to the hotel.

Back in Fuengirola she positioned herself at a table outside a café facing the apartment. She bought herself a cool drink and kept an eye on the tower looking for a familiar face from the photographs that had been sent to 'Luciano'. Then the unexpected happened. She developed a headache and began to feel sick and increasingly uneasy. She squinted over at the apartment, the keys heavy in her pocket but could not bring herself to get up and walk the small distance to the tower that housed the apartment. Whether it was jet lag, food poisoning or nerves, the full weight of what they had planned came crashing down on her. She didn't want to go into a stranger's apartment and poke around his things. What was the point? She got up and went back to her hotel, lying for a while in her air conditioned room before packing up her things and booking out.

Engle flew back to Ireland and spent some more time getting to know her way around Ennis. Then on 4 September she got the plane home with some relief. She had picked up a lot of information but the outcome Collins had been hoping for did not come to pass. Howard, Robert and Niall could sleep soundly in their beds for a few more weeks untroubled by the plot unfolding around them. For the conspirators, though, it would be back to the drawing board. The plot had another act to unfold but before it could they needed another prop to convince their marks of their sincerity.

CHAPTER 10:

RICIN ROULETTE

Engle arrived back in Las Vegas, having gathered some useful information as well as the keys, but it would take some convincing if Collins was going to continue to play along. Communication had dried up for the moment, and trust would not be restored until there was proof that 'Luciano' and his team were up to the job.

Engle would later say that she was a willing participant in the manufacture of a poison that was intended to kill the Howards. She described how, sometime before she and Eid travelled to Ireland for the culmination of their plot, they made poison in their garage and set in motion a chain of events that would lead to one of Ireland's first bioterrorism alert. She said that at some stage in September 2006 she and Eid gathered together some castor beans and a drum of acetone bought over the internet through Lisa's Paypal account and, using standard kitchen appliances, attempted to manufacture one of the most dangerous toxins known to mankind.

Ricin has developed something of a celebrity status over the years. Biological warfare has taken on a new and sinister enormity since the attacks on the World Trade Centre in 2001. Not since the long dark nights of the Cold War has the world seemed so scary and terrorism become so widespread. Suddenly people became aware that the kind of subterranean chemistry experiments that had been doing the rounds since the 1960s could now be uploaded onto the internet and made freely available. Information that was one step away from urban myth took on the currency of terror and became something that would hold up in court. As the recipes of kitchen terrorism took on a darker respectability, would-be assassins tried them out, and again and again they hit the headlines. Out of all the half-baked and factually inaccurate recipes uploaded onto the internet, ricin was the one that made the most headlines.

Ricin comes from the castor bean; the same nondescript small brown bean that produces castor oil. The substance is a naturally occurring toxin that's present in the bean before it germinates. It could be there as nature's way of deterring hungry birds to give the bean the best chance to become a shoot. Certainly it's not the only bean that would have a nasty effect on the stomach in its natural state. Even the humble red kidney bean contains a similar but less lethal protein that can cause a nasty stomach upset if the bean is eaten raw.

Ricin is much more potent, however. It's estimated that it would only take an amount of the pure poison the size of a grain of salt to kill an adult human. It would take around 100 grains of arsenic to produce the same result. Add to this the fact that the castor plant is a popular decorative shrub and easily available. It's grown in gardens and as a house plant and in parts of the United States it grows wild. You can buy the seeds from any garden centre and they're freely available online. The thought that something so deadly could be growing happily at the bottom of your garden is an attractive thought for the more homicidally inclined mind. It's handy then that the recipes that are freely available online are so simple that anyone can make them.

Ricin makes a perfect poison for various reasons. It has no antidote and cannot be detected in the victim. There is no telltale scent or distracting taste to alert the target and death is almost guaranteed.

The only two substances nastier are plutonium and botulism. It might only make up between 1% and 5% of the castor bean but it would only take swallowing around half a dozen beans before you would be in serious trouble. It is estimated to be, gram for gram, around six thousand times more poisonous than cyanide and around 12,000 times more potent than rattle snake venom. Once it gets into the blood it makes the red blood cells clump together and eventually burst as they die. It also causes haemorrhaging in the intestinal tract and irreparable damage to the livers and kidneys. It's this action that has led to it being used successfully in the treatment of cancer. The ricin is made to bond with an antibody which can seek out the tumour cells, delivering the ricin to have its devastating effect. This isn't generally the way ricin makes the headlines though. It's the effect on the human body when the toxin doesn't have any benevolent antibodies steering its route that has earned it its reputation. A fatal poisoning with ricin means a slow and painful death with no hope of reprieve. All doctors are able to do to assist the victims is to make them as comfortable as possible.

Despite its toxicity, ricin has limited use as a so-called weapon of mass destruction.[1] During the Second World War, both the Americans and the British explored the development of a ricin bomb but they couldn't get beyond the fact the bombs generally have to explode and proteins like ricin don't react too well to extreme heat. More recently, ricin was found stockpiled by Saddam Hussein whose scientists had been exploring new ways of weaponizing it. The Iraqi regime declared eleven litres of the toxin but stated they had given up on the idea of mass dissemination in the early 1990s. It's widely accepted that the most effective way of weaponizing the toxin would be to make it into a fine spray but this has proved a lot more difficult than it sounds. In fact, despite the toxin's high media profile and undoubtedly lethal properties, the American authorities acknowledge that it is unsuited to mass attacks and its main power lies in terrorising the populous rather than decimating it. Even so, ricin still has an impressive reputation as a tool of assassination and a strong online mystique. Presumably this was behind its selection for use in the 'Lying Eyes' conspiracy, but despite its semi regular appearances in the news and the media frenzy surrounding it, as a tool of international espionage it is somewhat underused.

1　　Although it is incorrect to call ricin a weapon of mass destruction, it is specifically banned by the Convention on Biological Weapons.

There is one confirmed assassination attributed to ricin poisoning. That death occurred at the height of the Cold War and is the stuff of spy novels.

Georgi Markov, a Bulgarian writer and dissident, became the only confirmed victim of ricin poisoning when he was stabbed with a toxic umbrella. It's not known who carried out the hit but in the summer of 2008 the case was reopened with the full cooperation of the now democratic Bulgarian government. The murder has passed into popular culture, much referenced by writers and artists over the past thirty years. But what is often forgotten is that Markov wasn't the only victim of a ricin attack that year. Ten days earlier a fellow Bulgarian dissident, Vladimir Kostov had also been shot with a ricin pellet in a Paris Metro station. However, on this occasion the sugar coating didn't melt and only some of the ricin got into Kostov's bloodstream. After a couple of days with a raging fever he recovered. So the famous ricin assassination technique that's gone down in history as sure fire and deadly actually had a success rate of 50%. While the high failure rate with the KGB's injection technique may have been simply to do with the fact that Kostov was wearing thicker clothes than the unfortunate Georgi Markov, it is in line with the experience of many plotters who attempt to make the toxin their chosen weapon.

Ricin might not have been on the list put forward by 'John Smith' when he was advising 'Tony Luciano' on the best way to kill but the twelve step recipe that had been downloaded promised a sure fire death from the results of an experiment that apparently needed no more than high school chemistry knowledge. It didn't matter that the toxin that had been chosen was, in all likelihood, completely unsuitable for the plan that had been agreed between Collins and Eid. If the plan was to be completed according to the emails then Robert and Niall Howard would need to die within 24 hours of their father. If ricin had been used they could have lingered on for three or four days, even possibly survived.

But ricin had nevertheless been chosen as the right toxin and would be made. Engle described the process in the evidence she later gave in court. She said that once the recipe had been found the order was put in for some castor beans and some acetone, the two major ingredients required in the recipe. On the day they decided to brew up the toxin, she said they dressed up in masks and gloves and put the castor beans on to boil. After a while they took the beans off the heat and painstakingly took off the skins. They then took the skinned beans and put them in a blender with some of the acetone and a mystery third ingredient and blended them. Once the ingredients were blended they were passed through a coffee filter to get rid of the liquid. The filter was left to dry and was then scraped to collect the white powder that was left behind. Engle estimated that, through this method, they gathered enough powder to fill both sides of a contact lens case. There was little or no excess. She told the court that Eid had brought the contact lens case with him to Ireland.

It seems extraordinary that such a deadly poison could be manufactured so easily using equipment no more specialised that a food processor and a coffee filter. The recipe that Engle described in her evidence is similar to countless recipes for ricin found through a quick internet search. Most of the time the recipes come from just two sources and both sources are flawed procedures for extracting ricin from castor beans.[2] They have circulated through cyberspace for years, being rewritten and tweaked but the basic chemistry behind them is the same, what they produce is essentially a castor bean mash rather than pure ricin, a substance with more in common with the castor oil cake that was used as a fertiliser in the United States for years than a laboratory grade toxin to be used in biological warfare. The resultant white powder does indeed contain ricin, in around the same concentration as it is found in the bean in its natural state.

In the end Eid was not convicted on the charge of conspiracy to murder, when the jury failed to reach a decision. Eid was neither convicted nor acquitted. It's impossible to say how much ricin was manufactured by Engle and Eid but they believed they had gathered enough to kill Niall and Robert Howard.

---

2   See globalsecurity.org's National Security Notes 20/1/2004 *The Recipe for Ricin: Examining the legend* by George Smith PhD.

CHAPTER 11:

BUSTED

It was several weeks before Collins had any further contact from 'Luciano' after Engle's visit to Ireland in early September. Then on Monday, 18 September 2006 the phone calls started again. The plan was still on. They phoned each other back and forth for a couple of days before the email arrived on Wednesday morning.

> 'Info, that's what I need from you and very important.
>
> 1: Robert's birthday.
>
> 2: Niall's birthday.
>
> 3: P.J.'s birthday.
>
> 4: The safe in Malaga's number (maybe the same number in Ireland).
>
> 5: Your birthday (sorry maybe it help).
>
> 6: Any number you think it help to use to open the safe there. Most people used number to remember and not to forget. We will do it as burglary but we do have this number it help a lot. How low will we go?'

It was a couple of days before Collins had the chance to reply. She was still in Spain and as she had warned earlier it wasn't as easy to get internet access there. There was none at the apartment. Finally on Friday she wrote:

'I'll try to find out the number of the safe but I can't make it look suspicious. For example, I ask for the number and then somebody breaks in and opens it—especially when I'm not there. What would I want it for? Anyway the dates you asked for are as follows [she supplied a list of birth dates]. I can't think of anything else but if I do, I will email you. Take laptop with you!'

It was time for the final trip to Ireland. Tickets were booked for Eid and Engle to fly back to Shannon, this time paid for with P.J. Howard's own American Express credit card. Collins kept the number in her wallet. She was the one who took care of all the internet banking and with the amount of travelling they did it was just so much easier that way. She had told Howard the wallet had been stolen sometime around the beginning of August, around the time Engle was around the resort. Certainly he never saw her with that purse again.

On the Saturday, Collins called Eid again to go over the last minute details. He and Engle were due to catch a plane the following day. It was almost time to make the final moves. On Sunday morning, Collins wrote again with some last minute information.

'Hi Tony, I couldn't get away. We have guests in again and it is difficult. It may be hard to ring you later but I will do my best without looking suspicious. The guys are at home—didn't go away—so they might be out locally tonight. I have tried to get in touch this morning but their phones are off—I will try again later. The code is as I said. Nothing else.'

She was getting nervous and it wasn't long before she wrote again.

'You should have all available information now. Difficult to make contact at the moment—visitors as usual. Will ring later—or email if it's possible to get away. Ok?'

But Eid and Engle were already on their way to Ireland. They touched down in Shannon Airport that afternoon and, armed with the foreknowledge of Engle's previous visit, headed straight to the car rental desk. It would have been too risky to use Howard's card details here, whipping out a piece of paper in full view of the girl behind the desk who might be curious about where the actual card was. In the end Eid used his own card for the light blue Hyundai Getz they hired. Like an old married couple, Engle handled the forms and took over the driving since she had some idea of where they were going.

This time they hadn't booked into a hotel in Ennis itself. The Two Mile Inn had looked suitable and had the advantage of being less expensive and anonymous as well, the kind of place frequented by travelling salesmen and tourists. It had seemed a good choice when they had booked it online, once again using Howard's credit card details. Technically it was in Limerick but it was on the way to Ennis, and handy for the airport. It was also secluded. They booked into Room 208 as a couple but Eid was quick to ring Lisa once they had settled in, who thought he was in Ireland alone. Eid could be a very conscientious husband and kept in contact throughout the trip—at least until his arrest.

That evening they took it easy after the long trip from the States. Engle would later say that on the first evening in Ireland they simply took a drive into Ennis. They went out to the Westgate Business Park to get a look at Downes & Howard while it was still bright. The following evening, they would have to steal the desktop computer that was worrying Collins so much. It should be a simple enough job. Collins had provided the alarm code and her directions were extremely detailed. She had also thoughtfully left the keys for the office under a brick at the back of a house on the Clare Road. The road was actually known as the Limerick Road on the signs but Eid and Engle had Collins's detailed directions. What they had no way of knowing when they found the house was that this house belonged to Collins's younger son, David.

When they arrived at the house on that August evening in 2006 the house was empty as promised. Of course, Collins had known it would be—she had done most of the negotiating on David's behalf, even stopping off while doing her internet searches for a hitman to organise the exchange of the contracts at the beginning of September. The keys were where they were supposed to be, under a concrete block at the back of the house where they had sat since before Collins had flown to Spain. The keys safely recovered, Eid and Engle headed back to the Two Mile Inn to get some sleep.

The next day they rested until the evening. The preparations had been done and it was a simple matter of waiting until it was dark enough to break into the office. They had come prepared with all the thoroughness of two people completely unused to this kind of adventure. Their suitcase was a dressing up box for cat burglars. Rather than opting for simplicity and stealth, the disguises were one step away from stripy tops and bags marked SWAG. They carried black leather gloves, Hallowe'en masks, a blonde wig and a black wig.

Engle would later give the following account of the break in while giving evidence in court. She explained that Collins had given them all the details they needed to remove the computer. When she arrived at the office that evening she had the keys and the codes for the alarm. The computer was sitting where it was supposed to be in the reception area. They only needed the hard drive so the monitor and the bulky cables remained where they were. Then there was ample time to have a look around the rest of the office. There was a blue Toshiba laptop in Robert's office. That was taken along with the power cables and the yellow (Ethernet) cable for connecting to the internet, as well as a digital clock. Then, finally, a souvenir of the adventure—a picture from the wall—a framed poster of the old Lady Lavery Irish bank notes. Taken out of its frame the poster could fold up small enough to fit under a jacket. It might not be legal tender, or even close to it, but it was a decorative thing, and a fine reminder of an Irish visit. Now laden with ill gotten gains, it was too much trouble to turn the alarm back on and close the Chubb lock on exit just over ten minutes later. At that time of night it also seemed a long way to the sea, so Collins's instructions were once again not carried out to the letter. Back at the Two Mile Inn it seemed simplest to dump the computers around the back of the hotel where they could remain hidden. The hard drive stolen from reception would remain here until it was located by a caretaker some weeks later. But Eid had other plans for the laptop.

After they had been back in Room 208 for a while, Eid decided to go back downstairs and bring up the laptop. The temptation to have a little bit of internet access was just too much. So the laptop came up to Room 208 along with its cables and the internet connection. Eid switched it on and checked the American football scores. Then he and Engle checked their emails as well as the emails for both 'Tony Luciano' and hire_hitman@yahoo.com. There had been no further contact from Collins and things needed to move along—so 'Luciano' was once again called into service.

> 'Call me ASAP. I not gonna wait here for nothing—I have to leave here by Sun morning.'

The next morning Robert Howard went into work as normal. He noticed the Chubb lock wasn't locked on the front door. When he went upstairs the alarm wasn't on, he knew that it had been when he and his brother had left the office the day before. He immediately saw that the desktop computer from the reception area was missing and on further investigation found that his laptop had been taken as well. He called the gardaí to report the robbery and once they had finally left he was able to go about his normal business. He had been running the business since his father had taken a back seat to spend more time in Spain, although Howard was the registered owner.

That evening Robert was back in the house he shared with his brother when the phone rang. It was around 10.30p.m. He answered the call without thinking. It had been a long and frustrating day and the brothers were finally relaxing in front of the television. But the voice on the other end of the line made Robert sit up and take notice. It was a male voice, not someone he recognised, he couldn't place the accent. The mystery caller asked him if there had been a break in at the office, and said he had heard Robert had lost a few computers. Robert, fully on alert now, agreed cautiously. The unidentified man didn't elaborate. He simply said that he would be at the house in about five minutes. Sure enough a couple of minutes later there was a knock on the door. Robert went to open it while Niall moved round to the window to get a look at the stranger.

Eid had decided to double cross Collins and offer Robert Howard the chance to buy out of the contract. He and Engle had decided to follow the same plan they had a couple of weeks earlier in California but they tried to improve on it in any way they could.

Engle was waiting in the car on the road as Eid walked down the drive to the Howard's house. He wouldn't make the mistake of giving his real name this time; he introduced himself to Robert as Tony when he opened the door. In the light of the window Robert thought the man in front of him might have been Algerian, even though once again Eid was claiming to be Italian. Eid hadn't dressed the part this time. He was wearing a tracksuit with a baseball cap pulled down over his eyes. Robert noted that the cap was embroidered with the insignia of the US Open golf tournament. He could see 'Luciano' was holding something on the bonnet of Robert's own jeep. He recognised his laptop. 'Luciano' handed it to him and watched while Robert brought it inside to his brother. He waited patiently until Robert came back outside and gestured for them to sit down on the step to talk.

Then he dealt his masterstroke. He told him about the contract on himself, his brother and his father in Spain. Robert was shocked. This sort of thing didn't happen in Ennis. By now Eid was on a familiar script and his natural flair for extortion came out once more. Without mentioning Collins for the moment he explained that the contract had been due to go ahead that week. He tailored the package for the particular mark. His price had gone up considerably since he had made the same offer to Lauryn Royston. He told Robert that the contract against him and his family had been for €130,000, a hike in the price he had quoted Collins that would have more than wiped out the $37,000 he hadn't managed to extract from Lauryn Royston.

He once again played the Mafioso with a heart of gold, saying he couldn't bring himself to carry out the hit. He offered Robert the knock down price of €100,000, still considerably more than he would have got from Collins if he had attempted to go through with her plan. Robert didn't know what to say, he was worried that this Tony was actually carrying some kind of weapon with which he could follow through on his threat if they didn't pay up. He needn't have worried. Eid was more in favour of a show and tell at these kinds of meetings not some kind of brute force. He showed Robert a selection of directions, directions that would bring someone to Robert's house, to Ballybeg House and even out to Kilkee, to the holiday home there that had seemed so safe. He even had the password for the laptop. He also produced the photographs Collins had sent, even the one of herself and Howard, the one where she had pointed herself out to him as the 'devil in the red dress'.

Robert took the proffered photographs, almost snatching them out of Eid's hand. There was his father standing proudly on the deck of the Heartbeat smiling down at his friend below. Eid argued his case for a while. They had been talking for around twenty minutes. At one stage, one of the two friends who shared the house with the brothers came home, stepping over the strange man on the step to get to the front door. She didn't notice anything odd, neither her housemate's nervous demeanour nor Tony's completely foreign exuberance. She would not be able to describe the stranger to gardaí when they eventually came calling.

Once she had gone inside Robert got up and took the photographs in to his brother. He showed them to Niall and told him to phone the gardaí, which he did using his brother's phone. But if he had expected the mysterious Tony to stay put and wait to face the music he would be disappointed. Niall moved into the side bedroom to see what 'Luciano' was up to outside while his brother was talking to the gardaí. He was just in time to see Eid walk off down the drive. The two brothers ran out of the house. Niall grabbed a pen and paper on the way out to note down the licence plate of Tony's get away vehicle but they were too late. They saw Eid hurry to the roadside and jump into a waiting car which sped off down the road with its lights off. The brothers ran back to Robert's jeep and gave chase but the car was too quick for them. They couldn't even get a clear look at it. Niall thought it might have been silver or maybe green but it was hard to tell in the sodium streetlights. They turned the car around and headed for home. Robert phoned his dad to tell him what had happened. Howard was alarmed but powerless in his Spanish penthouse. Robert was still talking to him when the gardaí arrived at the house.

For the second time that day Robert found himself giving a statement to the gardaí. They told him to keep in touch and left. The brothers settled back down to what remained of their evening but it wasn't long before the phone rang again. It was now around 12.30 a.m. Eid hadn't been able to let things lie until the morning and wanted to make sure his visit had had the desired effect. He stopped at a pay phone in Limerick city on the way back from the hotel—he wanted to get things concluded as quickly as possible and he knew that these marks actually had serious money at their disposal.

How long could it take them to raise the money? He must have been basing his assumptions on the gangster movies he was so fond of. He got straight to the point asking Robert if he had started getting the money together yet? Playing for time Robert told him that he had but wouldn't have the whole amount until the following day. Eid said he would ring back in the morning and they would arrange an early meeting.

Sure enough the next day Robert's phone rang once more. It was Eid in 'Luciano' mode. He once again asked if the money was ready. Robert hedged the answer a little but didn't deny it. We'll be in touch he was told. Wait for our call. So he waited … for most of the day. He told the gardaí what was going on and they told him to play along, while they mounted their own surveillance operation. Robert was scared, he had no way of knowing what 'Luciano' would do if they didn't pay up. Just as Lauryn Royston had feared for her life, Robert was convinced that the threat was real. He rang a local security consultant to ask about getting a bodyguard for himself and his brother. He was glad that his father and Collins were safely out of the country. Finally at around 4.45 p.m. 'Luciano' rang again. Eid had picked one of the few places they had some local knowledge about—the Queen's Hotel, Engle's first base in the Ennis region. He gave Robert his instructions like something straight out of a spy novel. Be at the Queen's Hotel in half an hour, come alone, bring the money. Robert did as he was told, with one amendment. Before he left to drive into Ennis he phoned the gardaí and told them the plan. By the time he reached the hotel there were ten plain clothes gardaí scattered around the hotel and the neighbouring streets. They were watching the car parks and every approach to the hotel. There was no way 'Luciano' was going to slip through their net without being caught.

Robert took a seat at the bar and ordered a drink. He waited nervously for his phone to ring. He was aware that there were two female gardaí in the hotel watching him and it was unlikely anything could go wrong but he was still worried. He barely noticed when Engle swept past him on her way to the toilets although something about her registered on the edge of his consciousness. Then finally his phone rang again. He grabbed it to answer the call and all around him the waiting gardaí got ready to make an arrest. It was Eid, sitting across the road in the Library Bar from where he could keep an eye on the proceedings. It was 5.40 p.m., almost an hour since his last call. Robert had been sitting at the bar for almost half an hour but finally it was show time. Eid told him to go towards the Ladies' toilets just beyond the bar in a small lobby area. A nice private space for the kind of transaction they were about to carry out. He would be met there by a woman. He was to give her the money and wait while she counted it. All nice and businesslike, as if they had done this successfully so many times before.

Robert got up and headed over. Engle followed close behind, once again chosen to be the one to collect the spoils of the game. They stood in the small carpeted lobby between the glass doors leading to the bar and the front desk. To their right he could see the reception area, muffled behind the second door, people going about their business completely unaware of the covert operation going on in their midst. Engle didn't waste time. She looked Robert up and down and noticed his empty hands. She asked him if he had brought an envelope for her. Robert was playing along as the guards had told him to. The computer first, he insisted, hardly missing a beat, after all there were two computers stolen and only one of them had been returned.

'Were you not talking to him?' Engle asked, her irritation showing as this extortion attempt looked set to go south just as quickly as the one in California. Robert held firm. He wanted the reception computer back, unaware that it would end up incriminating Collins. He asked to speak to 'Luciano'. Realising that this attempt too was going to end in failure, Engle brushed past him and walked away. She didn't see the gardaí who followed her from a discreet distance behind. Eid came out to meet her. From where he was sitting he could see her leave the hotel. Engle told him what had happened then headed back to the car, parked a short distance away. The gardaí were waiting for her. Eid stopped off at a phone box and once again rang Robert, trying to salvage something from what was rapidly becoming a very expensive trip for nothing. He asked him what he was playing at. Why hadn't he handed over the money? Robert was getting into his stride by now, no computer, no money he insisted. Eid hung up the phone, the conversation hadn't gone the way he had hoped. To be honest this new attempt was going no better than the last. As he stepped out of the phone box the gardaí swooped. This extortion was going considerably worse than the previous one.

Both Eid and Engle were taken to Ennis garda station for questioning. Eid said nothing of any importance but Engle began to confess and was quick to tell the gardaí that she was simply another victim in all of this. She was merely Eid's pawn, an unwilling partner in all the subterfuge. He had been keeping her a virtual prisoner in the States, all she wanted was a chance to get away from him. Her voice was whispery and timid and she looked gaunt and stressed. The detectives interviewing her had no doubt that she would make a good witness, despite her position.

Eid, on the other hand, was unhelpful when it came to answering questions, his manner alternating between irritated belligerence and incredulous jocularity. He had only been on holiday with his wife. He didn't understand what all the fuss was about. What was all this about Tony? He wasn't Tony, his name was Essam. Nobody had mentioned Essam so they couldn't have been talking about him, could they? What about the things they had found in his hotel room? Eid still played dumb. What things? The cables from Robert Howard's laptop, the poster of the old bank notes, and digital clock that had been stolen. Eid looked at the clock. It was a nice one, wasn't it. Cool! He wasn't so impressed with the poster. What was the use of that? It wasn't even legal tender. They told him they knew the stuff was stolen. Eid was adamant. He didn't know anything about any office. It was a cool clock though. What about the wigs and the masks? Well it was almost Hallowe'en! The black gloves? Ireland was cold if you were used to the desert heat of Nevada. The detectives showed him the photographs he had brought with him to Robert's house. The photograph of P.J. Howard on his yacht and the other one of Howard with Collins sitting on his knee. They asked him did he recognise anyone in them?

Eid looked at them carefully. Oh yes he recognised them all right. The woman was Collins. It was at that point he said he was having an affair with her. The gardaí jumped on the suggestion and Eid warmed to his story. They had been having an affair for ages! He had even visited her on P.J. Howard's boat—when Howard wasn't there of course. He had been supposed to be travelling on to see her at the end of this visit, he told them, except Engle had insisted on tagging along. The gardaí weren't convinced. When they checked with Collins she was convincingly scandalised. The very idea was idiotic. But while the gardaí might not believe Eid's story of clandestine love, it was still the first time Collins's name had been raised as anything other than a victim in the whole extraordinary mess.

The interviews with Eid were going nowhere because he would not admit to anything. It was time to organise an identity parade. It was almost midnight on a midweek night when the gardaí started scouring the pubs of Ennis to rustle up a suitable line up. Eid began to cause problems in that regard. There weren't that many middle aged Egyptians in the town at any time of the day but at this time of night … they ended up making do with a motley assortment of locals, not an ideal selection but the Howard brothers still had no difficulties in picking Eid out of the line up.

Robert also had no difficulty picking out Engle as the woman he had spoken to during the meeting outside the toilets in the Queen's Hotel. The gardaí didn't doubt that she was every bit as complicit as Eid in the scam, but could not hold her. On 1 October, after three days in custody, she was allowed to board a flight back to the States. Back in Nevada she went straight back to the house on Camden Cove Street. She wasn't planning on staying. She wanted to put as much distance as she could between herself and Eid and it wouldn't hurt to get out of the way if the Feds came knocking about the California case.

Lisa was there when she called. They didn't have much to say to one another. Lisa kept asking her what was going on. Why had she and Eid been arrested? Why hadn't Eid been let go as well? Eventually Engle told her the truth. She told her about the website and the plot to kill the three Howard men. But there had never been any intention to kill anyone, she insisted. It was only ever going to be a hustle. Engle told Lisa about the stolen computer and the attempted extortion and finally a potted history of the arrest. She didn't stay long in the house, just taking the time to pick up some things. She wanted to go back to her family and maybe even to Todd, for a third time perhaps.

Back in Ireland, Eid did not have the opportunity to plan his future. The detective team who investigated the case did not believe a word he said. Engle had neatly sidestepped the consequences but the gardaí were still keen on Eid providing them with some of the answers they were lacking. He was furious that Engle had been let go. He felt he had been set up, plotted against by the women in his life. It hadn't all been down to him. Why should he be the only one to face the music? The gardaí wanted to keep him close; he was remanded in custody to Limerick Prison on theft charges.

Nothing about the case made any sense to the gardaí tasked to investigate the extortion attempt. None could understand how Eid had obtained pictures of P.J. Howard and why he had said he was having an affair with Collins.

Collins was back to being the model partner and spending most of her time with P.J. Howard. Engle had disappeared into the bosom of her family and things seemed to be going well with the ever faithful Todd. The only thing she hadn't done was fess up to her little misdemeanours in California. The FBI were very interested to talk to her in relation to Lauryn Royston's complaint but when Engle went to ground she wasn't that easy to track down. She hadn't even left a forwarding address with Lisa. She wanted to put as much distance between herself and Eid as she could.

Eid wasn't going to let her go that easily though. He was, of course, still in contact with Lisa, his lawful wife who, for the time being, was standing by her man. On 1 December he persuaded her to send Engle an email from his account pretending to be him. Lisa did what he asked. She wanted Engle out of their lives as much as he wanted her to take the rap. She wrote asking Engle for the rings he had given her when they had their Vegas wedding. Engle also wanted out. She wrote back quickly promising to send them back. All was charm and affection; the two women played their parts as they had done for Eid so many times before. Engle wrote back to Lisa playing Eid, wishing her 'good luck and have a nice life.' She didn't ask how things had gone in Ireland. Lisa didn't offer any information. She wrote back to the woman with whom she had shared her husband, 'I wish you good health and happiness.' So things ended on an amicable note. But this wasn't getting the result Eid wanted. A couple of weeks later he persuaded Lisa to write from his email address again. This time his plan was to set a trap. He told Lisa what to write. On 14 December she wrote,

> 'I'm in New York just from Paris on my way to Chicago to visit Aya. If you want to meet somewhere email me back ASAP.'

The plan was to tip off the Feds once the meeting was arranged. He wasn't going to be the only one facing a prison sentence. Engle once again replied quickly. Maybe the last time she had sensed that it wasn't Eid on the other end of the keyboard. Maybe she wanted to twist the knife a little in the other woman. Either way she wasn't going to play ball. She wrote back a single line.

'I dreamed about you last night. I can't seem to get you off of my mind.'

She didn't fall for the meeting. Perhaps she knew that it was unlikely Eid would walk away as she had. Especially after she had convinced the gardaí what a monster he was. It would take a little longer for the FBI to finally track her down to her family home where she had gone back to living with her sister and daughter, her flight to Las Vegas forgotten in her hour of need. Eventually though, Eid had the satisfaction of knowing that he wouldn't be the only one to face the music. Although once again, Engle would charm the authorities with her story of abuse and coercion. She agreed to cooperate fully with the FBI, all the better to make sure Eid bore the brunt of whatever punishment was heading their way. She agreed to tell them anything they wanted and plead guilty to her part in the California case. She was really just another victim in all of this after all. As 2007 began, Engle started helping the FBI. She proved to be a particularly informative witness. She told them details that began to close the net not just on her lover, but also on 'Lying Eyes' herself.

CHAPTER 12:

FIND THE LADY

Yet for several months it seemed that Collins had got away with it. The Advent computer had disappeared without trace, and the gardaí had no proof whatsoever of her involvement with Eid though they were deeply suspicious of her. Howard was standing by her and life was continuing pretty much as normal. No one had believed the claim that she and Eid were having an affair. She claimed that she had been the intended victim of an elaborate fraud.

Then her world collapsed. The FBI conducted a search of 6108 Camden Cove Street looking for documents that would provide them with a link to the website that advertised 'Luciano's' dubious services. They left with a blue plastic folder in which someone had thoughtfully stored an enticing range of documentation.

There were emails from Collins, internet booking forms for trips to Ireland and a letter from Eid's boss at the Bellagio confirming he worked there for the purposes of a visa to Ireland. Whoever had been keeping up the correspondence had been very conscientious about keeping records. There was far more here than the FBI was actually looking for. They had gone in searching for documentary proof for the extortion attempt on Anne Lauryn Royston. What they came out with was a tantalising glimpse of a plot that stretched across the Atlantic.

They notified the gardaí who notified Collins that they would be needing to talk to her on a somewhat more formal footing. Collins was in bed when they arrived on 26 February 2007. She didn't hear them immediately as they let themselves into the open door of Ballybeg House shouting her name. She came out of the bedroom in her nightclothes as they were coming up the stairs. A female garda stayed with her while she got dressed despite her protestations that she was perfectly happy to go to the garda station herself.

She didn't seem to understand the change in her circumstances—it was eventually explained to her that as a suspect it wasn't up to her to go to the gardaí. From now on the gardaí would always come to her and they would continue to do so until she answered their questions to their satisfaction. So began an interview process that must have been frustrating for all concerned. Collins stuck to the story she had told P.J. Howard in the wake of the robbery. It was a tale of a woman called Maria Marconi; a tall blonde with more than a passing resemblance to a young Lauren Bacall and an effortless sense of style. To a cynical observer it might seem that Maria Marconi was not just an alibi but an idealised alter ego created by an ultimately insecure woman.

The gardaí asked her if she meant Engle by her description but Collins scornfully dismissed the idea, even though the description of the elusive Marconi differed from that of Eid's former lover only on the matter of hair colour and style. Collins described in detail how her writing mentor Marconi had come to visit her in Clare in June 2005, after Collins had been writing exercises for her for months. She said that she had been in Spain when Marconi rang to tell her she was coming to visit Ireland but her visit home had corresponded with her arrival in the area. She said she met Marconi at the Downes & Howard offices and Marconi had asked to use the computer. While she was checking her email she had somehow managed to hack all the computers she had access to—setting Collins up like a rat in a trap.

She wove an alibi that ticked every box in the case the gardaí would eventually put together. She described the car trip that had taken Marconi around Clare. She explained how she had taken the scenic route, pointing out all the places she had written about in her writing exercises, how they had visited Kilkee and had ice cream—only a small one for her because she was dieting. She told of a quick visit to Ballybeg House where Marconi had needed to use the bathroom and had been shown to the en suite off the master bedroom. The detail was drawn with an imaginative eye, almost a novelist's attention to detail, keeping her story just close enough to the truth to keep in sync with what couldn't be brushed away as coincidence and she stuck to it.

Marconi, she said, had returned to the States but had soon been in contact again. She rang while Collins was in Spain, very upset. She said that her apartment had been broken into and among the things stolen was the laptop she used to keep in touch with all of the would-be writers she was mentoring, Collins included. Collins said Marconi warned her that all the emails they had sent each other were stored on the laptop but she had not thought any more about it. It was not until she had started receiving bizarre junk mail that she began to get worried, she earnestly told the gardaí. She said that she had deleted the first couple of emails without reading them but then one arrived with her name at the top. It told her she could be set for life if she wanted to be but wasn't very specific about what that entailed. Collins told them the phone calls started soon after, growing increasingly threatening as she listened in disbelief to the threats. She said she couldn't remember if the calls had all come from the same man or whether he had any kind of accent. She thought it was an American accent and had she mentioned that it could have been Marconi's boyfriend.

The phone calls had frightened her anyway, whoever they were from. They said they had all Marconi's emails, including a particularly nasty one Collins had written about her partner. In this email she had made allegations about P.J. Howard's sexual preferences. Now the mystery man or men were threatening to email the incriminating emails to Howard. She was terrified. She knew how much it would hurt him if he found out the kind of things she had been telling other people about him so she agreed to pay €15,000 to the blackmailers. She didn't know why the blackmailers were using Essam Eid's address. Those were just her instructions.

Collins refused to acknowledge she was being treated like a common criminal, she insisted on treating the interviews like a rather awkward social occasion. She resolutely called the guards by their first names, making firm eye contact and smiling at the absurdity of the situation. She held a white handkerchief clutched in her hands which she kept patting smooth on her knee before folding it over and over on itself as she thought furiously for a way out. As the interviews slowly progressed the tissue was folded and unfolded countless times but Collins never stopped talking. The guards struggled to keep up, but had great difficulty keeping notes of the rapid-fire stream of stories that Collins was providing them with. She complained they hadn't managed to capture her 'tone of voice' in their notes and had missed out swathes of what she was telling them, how could their paraphrasing put across the whole truth? She wanted it word for word otherwise it wasn't truly what she said. She would frown as the garda notes were read out to her at the end of each interview, then every time a new interview started she would lean forward earnestly and voice her concerns. It just really didn't sound like her.

Over hours of interviews that February, she fleshed out her story. Marconi became a living, breathing person whose aim in life was to ruin everything Collins had built up over the years. Collins said she was the victim in all of this, herself and her family; all of her family. She had been like a mother to the Howard boys, she would never do anything to harm them. Over almost three days she denied and denied, and wept and laughed and tried to make the detectives understand that it was all some kind of horrible mistake. For their part, the gardaí only had Eid's word that there had been a link between him and Collins. They hadn't had time yet to forensically examine the Iridium laptop they had taken from Ballybeg House when they went back to search it after Collins's arrest and the computer from Downes & Howard was still missing.

At that stage the gardaí hadn't yet found the emails on both computers or discovered the fact that Collins's computer profile for the Iridium laptop had been wiped two weeks later than she had claimed, when the heat had started getting a little bit too hot and gardaí attention had started to be turned in her direction. For the moment they simply didn't have anything else to go with.

In the US, Teresa Engle who was 'helping' the FBI with their investigation about the Royston case, was being far more forthcoming about that case and about events in Ennis as well. The gardaí had travelled to and from Nevada and the case against Eid was shaping up nicely. But there hadn't been much movement since the February interviews with Collins. Then they received information that could provide the proof they were looking for.

Reminiscing about their stay in the Two Mile Inn Engle told Special Agent Ingrid Sotelo how they had dumped the heavy desktop computer in a wooded area around the back of the hotel. It could still be there. The FBI promptly told the gardaí where the hardware was to be found and the gardaí dispatched a team to recover it from the bushes, hoping against hope that an Irish winter hadn't reduced the hard drive to useless junk and they could find that vital proof.

The winter of 2005 had been a mild one. If the desktop had remained in its hiding place it would certainly have been damaged by the rain and what frost there was, and the incriminating emails from 'Lyingeyes' could have been lost forever. Luckily for the gardaí, the hard drive had been found long before the worst of the winter took hold.

Christie Tobin had been the caretaker at the Two Mile Inn for years. It was his job to oversee the general maintenance of the hotel and see that any technical hitches the guests encountered were sorted out. When he wasn't needed he spent most of his time in his workroom deep in the bowels of the building. He was a solid Clare man who didn't waste his words and didn't see the point of bringing things up that weren't asked about.

One of his duties was to check around the outside of the hotel to see if the guests had left anything behind. It was amazing what was left behind or abandoned in the bushes round the back. Tobin set off on his tour of the bushes expecting to find cumbersome rubbish that would be gathered up and put in a skip to be disposed of. It was autumn and the weather hadn't grown cold just yet. The Advent computer was wrapped up in a black canvas bag. The bag had successfully protected it from the worst of the weather and the hard drive looked just as it had in the offices of Downes & Howard.

When he found the computer, he took it, bag and all, into his workshop and stowed it away. He made enquiries to make sure none of the hotel computers had found their way into the bushes for whatever reason but none were missing. It wasn't until all his research had drawn a complete and utter blank that he began to look on the Advent as his own. Eventually he decided to check it was working and plugged it in. The hard drive whirred into action but without a monitor it was no use so he unplugged it and zipped it back up into its bag. He left it stored in his workshop for safekeeping, should the owner come forward. It was still sitting in the corner of the workroom when Detective Jarlaith Fahy came looking for it on 24

April 2007. Tobin recounted how he had found it and put it away for safekeeping and then handed it over without complaint. He was more than happy to help. The crucial hard drive was rushed off for further examination.

Meanwhile, Collins was not taking the accusations against her lying down. She was the kind of woman who was used to being able to talk her way out of anything and she believed she could do so again. Once again she turned to the internet to find a way out. She researched where things were likely to go from here and learnt that she had the right to make a personal appeal to the Director of Public Prosecutions (DPP). Well, if anyone could persuade the DPP not to consider pressing charges she believed she could. This was nothing more than wishful thinking, and also displayed a slight arrogance on her part; that she believed she could achieve things that no one else could.

So in March, against the advice of her solicitor who knew that the letters could and would be read out in court if she were charged, she wrote the first of three letters to the DPP.

In a bright conversational tone she described her predicament and explained what a huge misunderstanding the whole thing was. She went into all the details of the Marconi visit and the subsequent blackmail attempt. After three or so pages she got into her stride and once again entered the stream of consciousness that had characterised her garda interviews. In her mind the Director, sitting in his Dublin office, aloof and all powerful, was her pen pal, her confident and her potential saviour. She poured her heart out in the way she said she had done with Maria

Marconi and had certainly done with the shadowy 'Tony Luciano'. Over almost a dozen pages she told the DPP all about her life in Ennis, her family, her relationship and all the convoluted details of her alibi. She begged him to let her go, casting herself as the tragic heroine in the story of her own telling. When the alibi had been spun in masterly detail it occurred to her the Director might think she was the kind of person who was capable of being involved in such a sordid little plot.

She wasn't like that, she insisted, she was a good woman, a religious, spiritual woman who went to the retreat on Lough Derg every year without fail. She had a strong moral compass although she believed in the death penalty and euthanasia and abortion. Though, she added hastily, the Director shouldn't think she was someone who was cavalier about taking a human life. She would never do anything to hurt her nearest and dearest. She just wasn't that kind of person.

She never received a response from the DPP. Luckily she hadn't been cast completely adrift since her arrest. P.J. Howard was standing by her. Since her arrest he had been her rock. Now he had another idea to help. He believed the story of Marconi as recounted by Collins; he simply could not accept that Collins would ever betray him. Marconi was a welcome scapegoat behind whom Collins could hide. If the ridiculous matter ever came to court she could be their star witness, that's if she could be found.

Collins didn't have any contact details for her though. She blamed a virus or a hacker and Howard, a typical man of his generation, didn't know enough about computers to argue with her. It might make things more difficult but what use was money if it didn't solve these problems when life threw them up? Collins thought Marconi might have had a connection to Eid; that would mean she came from Las Vegas. Howard bought Collins an open return ticket and sent her to Nevada. Collins flew over and spent around ten days investigating the mythical figure. She was determined to find the woman whom the FBI had failed to find. By the time Collins got home to Howard she had hired Venus Lovetere, who she asked to find Marconi who would prove her innocence.

Meanwhile the gardaí had been busy analysing the various computers seized on both sides on the Atlantic. The extraordinary correspondence between Lyingeyes and 'Tony Luciano' was revealed piece by piece. The emails were peppered through the hard drives of the computers. The correspondence was scattered but easy to put back together. The Advent hard drive that Christie Tobin had found yielded up searches for hitmen and assassins, contract killers and inheritance rights. Collins had known this was possible and had begged for it to be removed and dumped somewhere irretrievable but the bumbling scam artists she had hired hadn't bothered. They had only got as far as the back of the Two Mile Inn and thanks to Tobin's work room the Advent hard drive was in perfect condition to give up its secrets. Collins had been right to be worried about the searches that had taken place but in the end it was not the searches 'Lyingeyes' had conducted for a hitman that made the biggest impact on the garda team, it was searches of a more mundane kind that sparked their interest.

Secure in the anonymity of a web based pseudonym Collins had emailed 'Luciano' far more freely than she should have. While the Las Vegas conmen were happy to constantly use the name Tony, Collins had used the name of Bernie Lyons to open the 'Lyingeyes' email address, and repeatedly signed her own name. She also used an internet search engine that provided an email address which stayed logged in when the user went back to the home page.

This showed that 'Lyingeyes' was researching Reductil slimming pills and astrological predictions for Collins's date of birth. No one would believe her story of a second person trying to trap her; an Irish accomplice ... maybe Maria Marconi didn't really live in Las Vegas after all. The material the forensics experts dredged out of the computer drives could have been explained that way but that would have required a desperation to believe that very few people had. As the picture became gradually clearer there was only one logical explanation—that Collins had absent-mindedly skipped between her Lyingeyes alter ego and her habitual preoccupations, flitting between the dark plotting, the film noir search for a contract killer and her next flights to join Howard in Spain. The gardaí were faced with someone who was either a cold-blooded fiend who had an unnatural detachment from life and love or a fantasist embarking on a dangerous daydream.

Then in April there was another development when they found ricin in Eid's cell in Limerick Prison. Engle had been keen to show the FBI her willingness to cooperate and had continued to sing like the proverbial canary. She had described how they cooked up ricin in their kitchen and told Agent Sotelo where to find the blender in the garage at Camden Cove Street. Eid would have still had the lens case she said. So the FBI once more rang the gardaí and the men in white space suits turned up to cause a break in the monotony of prison life. Eid and his cell mate were banished from their cell and a full search was conducted. Eid would deny pointing the gardaí to the exact position of the lens case but they found it quickly nonetheless. The small flat case was found in a wash bag under his bunk. It was empty, except for a slight yellow stain at the bottom of one of the wells. Whatever it had once contained had been flushed long ago. Field tests signalled the presence of the deadly toxin, however.

The empty lens case was wrapped in a cocoon of plastic bags and loaded onto a waiting military jet with all due care and attention. Accompanied by senior members of the gardaí it flew through the night to England to an ex-government lab that has expertise in toxins. In the end the tests were done in a veterinary lab although the sample of pure ricin was provided by the secretive commercial lab, LGC, formally the Laboratory of the Government Chemist. Once again ricin was detected and the diagnosis was flown back to Ireland, although the contaminated lens case was locked away in the safety of the lab. No one argued. This put things into a whole different category.

Collins was unaware of this development. She had been staying in Spain while Howard made sure everything was all right back home. She found out about the ricin when Howard called her, after seeing it in the papers. It suddenly made the idea of a murder plot seem serious and all the more deadly. Howard was still standing by her but she decided she would return home. Howard met her in Dublin and tried to reassure her. Collins could feel things were getting out of control, so she wrote a second letter to the DPP. She explained her predicament and the lethal jail cell find, and explained that the longer this nastiness was hanging over her head the more stress it was putting on her family. She told the Director, who she now addressed with the familiarity of a pen pal, that she was not the kind of woman who would ever have anything to do with weapons of mass destruction, no matter what the papers might be saying. She pointed out that a lot of the press reports had been wildly inaccurate. They had been saying she was American for one thing, it didn't reflect what was going on at all. She hinted darkly that she was being set up. She didn't want to name names but there were people at home who wanted to hurt her. She was the victim of a sting far closer to home than any internet plot.

The guards had continued gathering their evidence. The computer analysis was taking time but a very clear picture of the plot was emerging. In June 2007 Collins was arrested again. She was still sticking to her story of Maria Marconi. She pointed out that Marconi might not have been American at all; she could have been locally based in Clare and able to have provided all the local knowledge that made the Lyingeyes emails so incriminating. She said she had also written exercises describing every aspect of her life. It wouldn't have been hard for someone only moderately creative to weave these details into the emails and make it look like it was her writing them. She had nothing to do with the plot; she had never met Essam Eid and never heard of a 'Tony Luciano'. The gardaí were unimpressed. They had found several things on the hard drive of the Advent computer that they felt would be extremely difficult to explain away.

Collins hinted that the blackmailers may have had an accomplice, and once again hinted that she knew who this could be. No one believed her story but they probed her to see what she would say. This was a game of cat and mouse. She wouldn't say that it was one of Howard's sons who had never wanted her to marry their father and now wanted her out of the way. When the gardaí suggested this to her she was indignant. She didn't want to accuse anyone wrongly when that was precisely what had been done to her. The gardaí suggested one of her own sons ... possibly David since Gary had been away in Australia at the time. They pointed out that it wasn't just Howard's sons who might have had a reason to want the relationship over, especially if they had any inkling of the allegations she seemed willing to tell to almost anyone. No one believed for a moment that the Howard brothers or her own sons would do such a thing. The detectives were testing her to gauge her reactions. She didn't take the bait.

Instead Collins reacted angrily—her sons would never do anything like that, and she could hardly blame Niall and Robert who she had wanted to kill. It was Maria Marconi and some man posing as 'Tony Luciano'. The gardaí, over hours of interviews, tried to make some headway but Collins wasn't budging.

The computer analysis had thrown up some very interesting irregularities though. They presented a photograph of Eid sitting in a bright yellow sports car, grinning at the camera. He was wearing large sun glasses and a baseball cap but was still recognisable as the man currently trying to explain the presence of a contaminated contact lens holder in his prison cell. It had been found on the hard drive of the Advent computer and corresponded to a description of a photograph sent to Lyingeyes by 'Tony Luciano'. Collins looked at the photograph with interest.

Wasn't that Marconi's boyfriend? He drove a yellow sports car she seemed to recall, it must be a photograph Marconi had sent her. No, she didn't know why there were no copies of the emails that had flown back and forwards between herself and Marconi. The ones sent to her Eircom email account had been deleted by a phantom hacker along with all the emails from the blackmailer. If they didn't believe her they could ask Eircom. She couldn't explain why so many emails sent to Lyingeyes had survived when a correspondence that had lasted for several months longer had disappeared without a trace. It must have been the Irish accomplice, someone with access to the computer at Downes and Howard. She couldn't say who. She wouldn't put someone else in the position she found herself in but there must be someone trying to set her up.

She berated Detectives Sergeant Michael Moloney and Jarlaith Fahy for putting her through the embarrassment of an arrest. She had nothing to hide, she said, she would have been completely happy to come in under her own steam. She wouldn't listen to their argument that it was more normal in an official investigation for suspects to be properly arrested and detained. She had her reputation to think of. The gardaí were not impressed. After all, by this stage they had also started an exhaustive examination of the impressive collection of phones that had been taken from Ballybeg house. Eid had at least three phones registered in his name and Collins had not made things easy either. She had a mobile for use at home in Clare and a separate one with a Spanish SIM to use when she was away with Howard in Fuengirola. Then there was the little used one registered in the name of Sharon Howard and a fourth registered to P.J. Howard, which he had used as a temporary solution while his normal phone was away being repaired. It had taken months and a bewildering array of requests from both Irish and American phone companies to get the full list of calls.

Then it was a matter of sifting through thousands of calls and finding the calls too and from the relevant numbers, but slowly a damning picture began to emerge. The gardaí found that not only were there phone calls that fitted neatly with the timing suggested in the Lyingeyes and 'Luciano' emails but another pattern was beginning to emerge. The emails already seemed to suggest that whoever had been emailing 'Luciano' had been not just following Collins's movements and possessing an intimate knowledge of her life but also was actually travelling with her. The phone records backed this theory up perfectly. Calls were made from the Irish mobile when Collins was at home in Clare and from the Spanish one when she visited Fuengirola. The calls also suggested a closer relationship with the blackmailer than Collins had been suggesting. There were calls lasting for almost half an hour at a time, more than long enough to allow for the flirtatious relationship obvious in the emails. The gardaí were beginning to think that not only was Collins their culprit but she was the only one who could have possibly made all the calls.

Feeling the evidence mounting up against her Collins wrote for the third and final time to the DPP. She made one last passionate plea to have her case dropped, it would cost those she loved far too dearly, she wrote. She said she was worried about David, always a sensitive child, whose epilepsy was threatening to re-emerge under all the stress he was under. She told the Director that David was taking her predicament harder than anyone.

But David wasn't the only one. She warned the Director that if he went ahead with the case against her he would be responsible for the deluge of misfortune that was about to strike her family. Howard was bound to keel over from his heart condition and her mother was well into her 70s. How could the Director be so cruel as to put an old woman through such an ordeal? She said that despite her views on the death penalty, euthanasia and all that she had always been opposed to suicide. It was not something that sat well with her Catholic spirituality. This horrible situation though, was putting her under so much personal stress that she had been reconsidering her position. If the Director went ahead with the charges he would be responsible for up to four deaths, three of them of people who had no accusations against them. Surely no criminal conviction was worth this high a cost in human life.

The letter was nothing more than an ill-conceived attempt to stop the investigation into her murderous conspiracy from proceedings. It was never going to work as the DPP would never entertain such dubious correspondence.

She even persuaded Howard to write as well. He duly wrote echoing Collins's passionate pleas. The woman he knew, who had nursed him through his illnesses would never do anything to harm anyone. His wrote that his Sharon was not the woman that she was being painted; she was a good woman and an honest one. When he wrote to the DPP he was not considering what a jury would make of his words. He only wanted the woman he loved to remain by his side.

The Director still didn't answer but it became obvious later that summer that Collins's pleas had been in vain. At the end of June, Collins was arrested and brought before Ennis District Court where she was charged with three charges of conspiracy to murder and a matching three of soliciting Essam Eid to murder P.J. Howard, Robert and Niall Howard. Essam Eid was also charged with conspiring to kill the three Howards and also had to face additional charges of demanding the money with menaces from Robert Howard, robbing the Downes and Howard offices and handling some of the items taken in that burglary.

But it was going to take the DPP far longer to prepare a book of evidence. At the end of August 2007, Eid's solicitor, John Casey, complained that his client had been locked up in jail since his arrest in September 2006, almost a year before. The incarceration had not been easy for the poker dealer who, despite his recent extra curricular activities, had no previous convictions. Eid was a diabetic and his condition was flaring up in jail. Casey warned the District Court judge that his normally cheerful client was becoming withdrawn and depressed and his health was deteriorating alarmingly. He demanded that his client's rights were recognised and asked the DPP to deliver a book of evidence or release Eid.

The DPP representative explained that an unforeseen problem had arisen but the evidence would soon be delivered to the defence.

Eid was to be sent back to his cell for another fortnight while the book of evidence was assembled. It was not an auspicious start for one of the most bizarre cases to appear before the Irish courts but, as happened throughout the trial, the DPP got it together and the evidence was produced although some of the finer points of the internet and phone evidence were not completed until the case had reached the steps of the Four Courts. The process had been put in place that would lead to a packed courtroom for nearly two months the following summer.

CHAPTER 13:

POKER FACE

On 21 May 2008 all the principals arrived for the final showdown. Collins's letters to the DPP had fallen on deaf ears and even Howard's pleas that she was innocent and didn't believe a word of the charges against her had failed to prevent the trial. Her threats of suicide and the decimation of her family had come to nothing and the only thing left for her to do was to try to and charm the jury. Wednesday, 21 May was the first day back after the courts' traditional Easter holiday. Court One, where all the juries for Central Criminal Court trials are sworn in, was packed with an airless pit of lawyers, gardaí, the accused and the general public, with members of the press pushing forward to hear what was going on. Hoards of barristers had gathered for the day to day business of the courts, looking after all the small legal difficulties that needed to be dealt with for a case to come to court.

The wooden benches were stuffed with the rather bemused jury panel, staring at the organised chaos exploding around them. Most were there unwillingly, just waiting for their chance to tell the judge why they couldn't do their civic duty. The rest were looking around anxiously, trying to spot the accused people among the throngs, trying to guess what story they would watch unfolding over the next week or so. They chattered amongst each other, trying to work out if any of the stories they had read in the papers would be presented for their entertainment. It might be an important part of the justice system but who wanted to waste a week or more watching something boring? Most of them didn't look in Collins's direction. In her smart black suit she looked like one of the solicitors. She was a small blonde presence flanked by her two sons, smiling easily while her solicitor stood a short distance away deep in last minute discussions with the rest of her legal team. For the jurors, glancing around the courtroom trying to ascertain the accused parties, she didn't even register.

For the reporters who had gathered together for the first time after the break, the main topic of conversation was not the petite blonde standing a short distance away, although several glanced curiously in her direction. The case had not yet registered in the media's consciousness. It had simply not rung the bells that usually ring in a trial that has the magic ingredients of sex and violence and the newsrooms were slow to get excited about a conspiracy that had failed to lead to a murder.

Even so, when the case was called and the two accused pushed through the throng to the front of the court to answer the charges against them there was a small murmur of interest through the courtroom. For the first time people got a look at Eid as he was led forward by two prison wardens. On pure face value he certainly looked the part. Collins half-heartedly stepped forward. Even at this early stage she certainly had no wish to stand beside her co-accused. They both stood and stared ahead as the ten charges were read out to them, allowing them to say whether they pleaded guilty or innocent. This was the first time the room had any inkling of the full extent of the allegations, but couched in dry legalese the full impact of the case still hadn't been made. It was then, once both Collins and Eid had denied all of the charges against them, that Tom O'Connell, the State's senior barrister, stood up and cleared his throat. He explained to Justice Paul Carney, the most senior of the judges who sit in the Central Criminal Court, and overseer of the jury selection for that court, that the jury had a right to know what they were letting themselves in for. It would be a complex trial and a long one. The State estimated it would take a month—in the end it would take almost double this. It might be an idea if he ran through the main points of the case so they knew what they would be facing. Justice Carney raised an eyebrow but nodded his consent.

O'Connell sketched out a potted history. He mentioned the fact that P.J. Howard was a wealthy businessman who divided his time between Ennis and the Costa del Sol. He told the suddenly silent courtroom that Collins was accused of hiring Eid to kill Howard and his two sons after her eight year relationship didn't look like it would pay out. Dozens of people looked at the small blonde who stared straight ahead and ignored the interest in the room. O'Connell told the room they would be hearing about a conspiracy that had started in the casinos of Las Vegas where the co-accused had a day job as a poker dealer. He mentioned the hitmanforhire.net website, the trail of emails, and demands for money with menaces. By the time he sat down the room was agog and the chances of finding a jury that would stay the distance had just gone up considerably.

Justice Carney warned the room that estimations on the duration of trials were invariably on the low side and the case would probably not finish until the end of June. With the holiday season about to start, it was with reluctance that several of the selected jurors stepped down. The legal teams refused others the chance to sit on the jury. In the end, eight men and four women sat in the padded seats of the jury box to be told they could select a foreman and get ready to begin. The trial itself would not start until the following day. Until then the three legal teams would start their negotiations, which would continue until the trial had passed the four week mark set by the prosecution, past the six weeks proposed by Justice Carney, to commandeer the entire term, eclipsing every other case that came and went in that period.

The next day it was standing room only in the court. Not because the masses had descended on the courtroom but because proceedings had started in one of the smaller courtrooms on the upper floors of the Four Courts complex. These rooms are usually used for civil matters, trials that are unlikely to require a lot of witnesses or public interest, where the more intimate surroundings suit the proceedings. The courtroom Collins and Eid found themselves beginning their trial in was No. 16, which was a small room on the second floor, often used to cater for cases of a sexual nature where the public are banned and the witness list tends to be small. The room is more modern and less imposing than the four courts that open off the Round Hall in the heart of the building. The windows are large and look down over the main gate onto the Liffey.

Although the traffic is muted by double glazing it gives an impression of a world outside, a less claustrophobic feel than the windowless wood panelling found in the main four courts.

The court is equipped with screens to allow younger witnesses to give evidence by video link, and the plain seating means that accused and witnesses share benches in absolute democracy. All these things give a slightly more relaxed feel to proceedings, less intimidating for the vulnerable. What the courtroom does not accommodate in any real or practical way are the hoards of witnesses needed in the average murder trial. All the eye witnesses and garda witnesses jostle for space with reporters sent to cover proceedings and the family of the victim, not to mention the accused and their family. When the trial is one where even the proposed victims are in attendance, space rapidly becomes limited. Eid sat next to the door with a prison guard sitting on either side. Past him sat Collins flanked now, as she was throughout the trial, by her sons Gary and David. Beyond Gary, sitting on the side closest to the windows, sat a few more gardaí, the senior detectives on the case. Then came the Howards, the victims of the appalling conspiracy, sitting beside the media advisor they had hired for the proceedings. They were surrounded by the reporters who had managed to fight their way to some seats. In the cramped surroundings the temperature was already rising rapidly as Justice Roderick Murphy took his seat.

Justice Murphy was best known as a judge in the civil courts. His attention to detail and thoroughness there was well known, but in the criminal courts he was something of an unknown quantity. His somewhat cautious and careful speech was unusual in the brasher environs of the Central Criminal Court. The two defence teams sat and waited since it was O'Connell who once again took the floor to make the opening speech for the prosecution.

In any criminal trial the format is the same. The prosecution opens the case and then calls witnesses. The defence have an opportunity to question witnesses as they see fit and have the option once the prosecution have finished putting their case, to call their own witnesses. After this both sides makes their closing arguments, with the prosecution once again going first. At all stages the accused are seen as innocent until such time as the jury feels the prosecution have proved their point and they decide to convict. Once the trial begins, everything is focused on the jury, everything must be explained so that the twelve men and women watching from the height of their jury box can understand the facts and the corresponding legal issues. It doesn't matter what the press write or say, unless it reflects badly on the accused and is deemed to be capable of influencing a conviction. O'Connell explained all of this to the jury before moving on to the facts of the case. Once again he outlined the main facts but this time went into a lot more detail. He described the robbery of the Downes & Howard offices, the taking of the two computers, the digital clock and the (rapidly becoming famous) poster of old bank notes. He gave an account of Howard and Collins's relationship, talked about the agreement not to marry and the impromptu ceremony in Sorrento before moving on to the 'reception' party in Spanish Point and finally the proxy marriage certificate bought off the internet. The emails between Lyingeyes and Luciano were read through to give an accurate idea of the depths of the conspiracy before the jury.

He highlighted the flirtatious tone, pointed out the reference to the devil in a red dress, ran through the main witnesses the jury could look forward to hearing from over the coming weeks. His speech went through the morning as the heat built in the small room, windows shut against the roar of traffic on the quays below. The reporters scribbled frantically in their notebooks while the accused in the story unfolding before the room sat stiff and still, staring straight ahead in the oppressive heat. By lunchtime he had just finished the emails recovered from the reception computer from Downes & Howard.

When the judge sent the jury to their lunch everyone got stiffly to their feet. The room emptied quickly as people poured into the corridor outside, enjoying the fresh air and the ability to stretch their legs. The broadcast reporters ran off to file for the lunchtime news; everyone else wandered off to lunch, slightly dazed from a morning of being bombarded with information, and there was a lot more to come.

After lunch the spectators gathered again, to be taken through the rest of the emails. Lined up against the back wall, squashed onto the only bench available for non legal people, the two accused sat uncomfortable close to their intended victims. Collins sat between her sons staring straight ahead at the judge. To her left, P.J. Howard sat, flanked by his two sons. They listened to the litany of evidence piling up against the woman who had been a good friend for so many years.

The opening speech then moved into the terms of the contract, the cut price offer of $90,000 for three lives. Neither the co-conspirators nor their 'marks' betrayed a flicker of emotion as the reporters glanced back and forth between them, looking for some colour for their evening copy. The hours dragged on. The heat built up again in the airless room; it was confirmed that the air conditioning was not working. Still the opening speech wore on. Then some time after 3 p.m. with the end in sight, the opening speech took a turn into darker waters. O'Connell had reached the ricin evidence. He proceeded to describe the search of Eid's cell in Limerick Prison and the finding of the contact lens case. The defence teams didn't look happy. This was contentious evidence even at this stage. It would be a greater problem later on.

O'Connell spent the rest of the day putting forward the prosecution case. It was an unusually long and detailed account of the evidence against the two accused but he explained that he wanted to give an impression of how strong a case the prosecution felt they had. The stories told by both accused were, he said, 'confabulation and lies'. By the time he had finished the courtroom clock was showing close to 4 p.m. and the day's proceedings were about to come to a close. The jury went home that night with an idea of what was to come. For Collins and Eid it must have been a daunting first day. There hadn't been a single witness yet, but the following days papers would paint a damning picture indeed. It was going to be a long trial.

The following day Robert Howard took briefly to the stand. It had been hoped that he, his brother and his father would finish their evidence in the first couple of days but in the end it would take several weeks to move past this initial account of 'Luciano's' Irish debut. Robert would take the stand no less than three times and it would be the following month before his father had finished his evidence. Collins's defence team would fight every aspect of the prosecution evidence, spurred on by her flurry of yellow Post It notes. She was going to fight this until the very end. Her future with Howard depended on it. Court 16 was still as hot and overcrowded as it had been for the opening speech. It was decided that one of the main courts on the ground floor would be better suited for the trial, which had already slowed to a snail's pace as both defence teams began their fight. In those early days, the jury spent more time sitting in their room away from the arguments that raged in the courtroom. It was going to be a very contentious trial. The first week ended as would many more during the course of the trial, with the jury being sent home early to allow the barristers to argue over the latest bone of contention.

The following week the court moved down to the Round Hall to one of the grand Gandon designed courtrooms. Space was no longer at a premium and the accused no longer had to sit on the same bench as their victims. Eid came in, laughing and chatting with the prison guards, and took his seat at the far end of the bench. Howard and his sons sat two rows behind the barristers, in the row usually occupied by victims and their families. Behind them the public galleries were full of reporters and gardaí, squeezed into the narrow wooden benches and craning forward to hear what was going on as the lawyers studiously ignored the microphones placed on their table to counteract the room's less than perfect acoustics. Already at this early stage, one or two members of the public had wandered in to take a look at the latest trial to hit the headlines. They winkled themselves in among the throng in the public benches.

On that first morning in the larger court, Collins and her sons also took their place in the public seats until the matter was brought to the judge's attention by David Sutton, Eid's senior barrister. He pointed out that it didn't look the best for his client if he was the only one directly in the jury's line of sight. It would seem that Collins was in some way less guilty, he argued. Collins ducked her head and muttered rapidly to her sons before looking imploringly towards her own legal team. Her own senior barrister, Paul O'Higgins took up the fight.

The court was treated to a brief lesson on the lack of a place for the dock in the Irish legal system. It was up to his client where she wanted to sit, he pointed out. She was, after all, perfectly innocent. Sutton countered quickly that at least his client had no problem looking the jury in the eye. Justice Murphy frowned as he considered the situation carefully.

'It might be fairer for everyone concerned if Ms Collins were to take her seat beside her co-accused so that both of them could face the jury in the full knowledge that they were innocent until a verdict was reached,' he concluded.

Collins reluctantly took her seat although it would be some time before the jury would again take theirs. The trial was to struggle on through several days of legal argument. Howard, Robert and Niall sat patiently in a row, waiting to be allowed to finish their evidence but they were only allowed to do so in fits and starts during the brief interludes when the jury were allowed into the courtroom. The rest of the time the arguments raged, while the Howards watched the barristers at their work. Collins sat facing them on the left. The place she had taken since that first day in the courtroom was level with the row where they sat, but she and Howard did not exchange glances. Collins's attention was taken up by her Post It notes, passed with increasing regularity down the row to her legal team. Howard sat with his sons and stared straight ahead. It was not until he finally took the stand a second time that members of the public could see whose side he was on.

P.J. Howard sat somewhat awkwardly in the witness box, looking down intently at O'Connell as he stood ready to question him. He was resistant to questioning from the off. Asked if he would count himself a wealthy man, with two luxury homes both mortgage free, Howard shook his head, refusing to agree that he was anything more than comfortable. He dismissed the proxy marriage certificate out of hand. He had known about it before the gardaí showed it to him, he said. The knowledge might have slipped his mind in the face of all their questions but Collins had thoughtfully rung him and pointed out that, yes, he had known about it for several months before they asked him. It would never have worked anyway, he said, his solicitor was well aware they had agreed not to marry.

The marriage certificate would have been completely useless and anyway, what would Collins have wanted with it, he stated noting that Collins had been absolutely fine about it when he had told her that any marriage between them would affect his children's assets.

His voice became more definite as he warmed to his subject. Collins was not a greedy person, she never had been, he said.

'In the eight years I have known Sharon she has never asked for anything. I have often offered her things and she has said no. If she's given three or four hundred euros for herself, she would see her two lads had enough. She would spend it on clothes and not save it. She is far from a greedy person,' he said.

He frowned as he announced to the court in general that he found it 'very, very, very hard to believe' that Collins would ever do anything like this against him.

'It just doesn't make sense to me at all; it's totally out of character.' This was why, he explained, he had sent her to Las Vegas to find a private detective to track down Marconi. Of course he believed her story, he said, she would never lie to him.

Had the private eye found anyone, O'Connell asked. Howard didn't miss a beat. He had a list, he said, a list of possible leads. He agreed that his credit card had been used to pay for Eid and Engle to fly to Ireland and stay in the Two Mile Inn. He also agreed that Collins kept his credit card details in her purse, because she was so much better at finding her way around the whole internet banking thing. It was easier to leave it to her to pay it online each month, he added. Her purse had been stolen before those flights were booked, and as far as he was concerned, she was in Spain at the time and had told him at the beginning of that September that her purse had been stolen.

'I have a strong reason to believe that Teresa Engle took that purse. She was there at the time. She was in Fuengirola staying in a particular hotel. She was supposed to be staying there for a few days and she disappeared I think after about one day. People said various things about why she was there,' he said.

He refused to accept any of the charges levelled against Collins and, when he was finally allowed to leave the witness box, he stopped by her, leaned down towards her, tenderly took her face in his hands and kissed her. He then whispered into her ear before walking out of the courtroom and out of the trial. The kiss remained one of the most talked about points in an extraordinary trial, sealing Collins's reputation as a femme fatale and Howard's as an honourable man who was standing by his partner because he didn't believe the allegations against her.

After the excitement of the kiss, things settled back down to the bad tempered norm. There seemed to be a problem with each piece of evidence the prosecution wanted to introduce and the battles would continue for hours in front of the benevolent adjudication of Justice Murphy. But no matter how strongly other points were argued the fiercest battle would come over the American evidence.

Engle was always going to be a controversial witness but with her testimony about the ricin cookery class and the plot to kill the Howards, she was vital to the prosecution case. Her evidence of making ricin with Eid gave the finding of the trace sample in Eid's cell a chronology it was otherwise lacking. As the barristers argued, she sat quietly in the public gallery, accompanied always by a female garda, since she was on bail. As well as her plea bargain she had also managed to obtain a letter from the Irish authorities saying that she had full immunity from prosecution. As the days dragged on in legal argument her nerves became ever more apparent. Eid was noticeably aware of her presence, knowing exactly what was coming if she took the stand. Every now and then, when there was a lull in proceedings, he would glance over but their eyes never met. At lunchtimes, when he had been taken back to his cell she would walk to a pub close to the court's complex, to push her food around her plate and frequently leave the table to smoke yet another cigarette. When she finally took the stand after almost a week of arguing about whether her testimony could be trusted or was admissable, it was to a packed courtroom. Everyone knew that after P.J. Howard, this was the main event, the most damning witness in the prosecution's arsenal.

Engle took to the witness box with a great show of humility. She hardly glanced at her former lover, all her attention focused on O'Connell as he gently led her through her evidence. She had put on weight since her arrest in Ennis, a sign to the gardaí that she was recovering from her virtual imprisonment by the poker dealer. Her voice was soft but sure as she calmly laid out every piece of incriminating evidence against Collins and Eid. She told how Eid had set up the hitmanforhire.net website, how she had not been involved with the site herself but had read all the emails from Collins. She had heard her speak on the phone as well. She said she could hear a strong Irish accent but no words; she knew that Eid had trouble understanding her and had to ask her to repeat herself, a fact born out by the emails. When she turned her attention to the ricin, the whole court leaned forward to hear. It wasn't often you heard the story of how someone had cooked up a biological weapon in their own house. Engle told the story well, her voice level as she explained that Eid had got the recipe from the internet. She said they had bought the castor beans and acetone online, and wore masks and gloves when making it. They used a blender and a coffee filter to make the toxin and had ended up with enough to fit in the contact lens holder. She described her trip to Ireland, how it had been with the intention to kill the two Howard brothers, Robert and Niall. The plan had always been to kill, she said. It wasn't just a con—those men were to die. Her voice shook with emotion as she told the courtroom at large, 'I am so very ashamed that I was involved in any of this.'

She insisted, however, that she had at all times been under Eid's complete control. By the time she had finished her evidence the outlook was bleak for both the accused. Then Paul O'Higgins stood up to start the cross examination on behalf of Collins. He pointed out that Engle was giving evidence under the shadow of her plea bargain under American law. Under the terms of the plea bargain, she had promised to give evidence. Surely, O'Higgins pressed, this meant that she was eager to please her new masters. If she didn't manage to impress them, and there were several FBI agents connected with the American investigation sitting in court watching her give evidence, there was no guarantee she would get the light sentence she was looking for, he stated. He held up as proof the fact that her sentencing had been adjourned until after she had given evidence in Ireland. Engle shook her head emphatically. She was only telling the truth. She said she had nothing to gain by telling lies. The American sentence was only adjourned so she could spend more time with her family before the inevitable jail time. O'Higgins was not impressed. She wasn't the shrinking violet she pretended to be, he told Engle. Had Eid been there when she told Joshua Hammond that he would be watching Lauryn Royston's burial if they didn't find the money she was demanding from them? he asked.

She had been under Eid's total control she told him.

Even when you were in another country? he further queried.

Yes, she had always been under his control. She had prayed to be arrested on that second trip to Ireland, just so she could get away from him, she said, adding that she had been trapped in America. Eid had made her sell her car and give up her job; he wouldn't even buy her cigarettes, or so she said.

'But you're back with your family now,' countered O'Higgins. 'You're back with the support of your sister and the twice married Todd Engle.'

'I'm not with Todd any more,' she insisted, 'but yes, I did marry him twice.'

She agreed she had neglected to divorce him before marrying Eid, when pressed by the barrister.

O'Higgins moved away from the subject of marriage to the matter of P.J. Howard's American Express card. Where had she got the details?

Collins had emailed the details to them before they had booked the flights to Ireland, she said. O'Higgins paused for a second before dealing his latest blow. There was no mention of the American Express in any of the emails. There were a lot of other numbers mentioned, safe combination numbers and alarm codes, but no credit card details. She had seen the email, Engle said.

'Can I suggest to you that all you are doing, far from wishing to tell the truth for its own sake, is seeking to advance your situation in the US,' he said.

Engle showed a rare flash of emotion as she countered, 'That's absolutely not true.'

He moved onto another point. The keys that Collins had supposedly left for Engle to collect when she arrived in Spain; the key's to P.J. Howard's penthouse apartment. Where had they disappeared to? Since neither she nor Eid had got the chance to make a return trip to Fuengirola, presumably someone had the keys.

Engle nodded; she had brought them with her. She said she had them on her when she was arrested. O'Higgins then posed a question that had the desired affect; if this was the case, why weren't they listed amongst her possessions when she was arrested. The gardaí listed $32, cigarettes, and a letter but no keys. No one had ever seen keys in her possession. She had got rid of them in the court house at Ennis, she told him. She had gone to the toilet, wrapped the keys in some tissue paper and dropped them into a bin. They might even still be there, she said. She looked directly at O'Higgins. She had come to this court to tell the truth, she told him.

'What I am saying now, I agreed to tell the truth against my attorney's advice here,' she said.

'What you say here has a major affect on what sentence you receive in the States.'

'I don't know about that,' she responded.

'Can I suggest that that too is a lie?'

He sat down and allowed David Sutton, Eid's formidable defence barrister, to take over. Sutton got straight down to business. Wasn't it true that Engle was the one person in this trial who had a criminal conviction? She had pleaded guilty to her part in the Californian case. Engle objected when he insisted on calling her a fraudster but admitted that she was certainly an incompetent criminal.

She agreed that her living arrangements with Lisa and Eid had been unusual to say the least after she had moved into the Camden Cove Street house in June 2006. He asked her who else had access to the computer there, or was it just used by Eid. No both herself and Lisa used it as well, she said adding that she would have had Eid's email passwords and so would Lisa.

Sutton was cutting on the subject of the ricin. They had simply cooked it up in the house? Did they test what they had made on anyone? Even a passing mouse? he asked.

Engle shook her head. Sutton went in for the kill by proclaiming they had never intended to kill anyone. It was all a scam, he said.

'Miss Engle, what that operation was all about was shaking people down, stealing and robbing them, not killing them,' he proclaimed.

'That's not what the website said.'

She insisted that the website should be taken at face value. She said the intention had always been to kill. Sutton was incredulous.

'This piece of nonsense?'

She nodded, thinking her point was made. 'That's what the intention was.'

The barrister glanced briefly around the room to be sure of his audience.

'The reason you are saying you intended to kill is that you are trying to do yourself a favour in America where you have pleaded guilty to another shakedown. You are dressing this up,' said Sutton.

Despite her protestations that the plan had always been to carry out the threats to kill, and it had only been Collins's failure to make contact that had commuted the outcome to a spot of extortion, the damage had been done. Even though, as she took her seat back in the public gallery, Eid looked into the crowd smiling and drew his finger across his throat in a jokily despairing gesture, Engle's credibility had been sufficiently dented to give the jury pause for thought.

The next couple of days seemed to underline the fact the hitmanforhire.net may have fallen short of delivering what it promised. The trial suddenly received a little Hollywood glamour with the arrival of a posse of FBI agents from the Californian investigation. There were detailed descriptions of the search of Eid's house in Las Vegas by agents who looked like actors from an American cop show, but it was the agent in charge, Ingrid Sotelo, who raised the most hackles among the defence counsels.

FBI Agent Sotelo, who was in charge of the Californian investigation, told the Central Criminal Court that she had come across the ricin residue on a visit to question Lisa Eid about Ashraf Gharbeiah. Engle had told her that they had made ricin the previous year and Sotelo decided to check out the information while she was at the house in Camden Cove Street. Lisa showed her through to the garage and pointed out a blender and coffee carafe that she said belonged to Engle.

Sotelo told the court that she could see the white residue from across the room. When she tried to take some photographs of the scene she discovered her camera batteries were flat, she said. She explained that Lisa stepped in and offered to use her own camera to take the shots and then email them to the FBI. Sotelo told her what to photograph and the Irish court was shown the photographs, although they were not formally entered as evidence.

Sotelo told the court that she had warned Lisa to stay out of the garage until the offending kitchen equipment was removed but said she took no further action as this would be outside her jurisdiction.

The barristers for the defence sought to find out why she had not thought to ensure that the local FBI branch in Nevada had done their duty, and cleaned up the traces of ricin from Engle and Eid's home. Sotelo, efficient and with a haze of blonde curly hair, was cutting as she tried to explain the peculiarities of federal jurisdictions. If she had seized any item from Eid's house, even with Lisa Eid's consent, she would have been breaking the law, she repeatedly explained. She had phoned it in when she got home to L.A. It wasn't any of her business what action was taken by the local FBI office.

But this was a deadly poison, the defence teams demanded, weren't you at least curious? Sotelo kept quiet on the subject of her curiosity, suggesting in her silence that puerile curiosity was not fitting for an FBI agent. Sotelo had brought a photograph of the tin of acetone she had found in the garage at 6108 Camden Cove Street. The photograph was shown to the court but not passed into evidence. The questioning went round in circles several times before a stale mate was reached and Agent Sotelo was allowed to leave the stand.

It was a welcome break in the tension to see Private Brian Buckley take the stand, bringing some much needed comic relief as his bafflement at being drawn into the trial radiated from the witness box.

'In the end I didn't see it as a joke. I didn't see it as serious either,' he said referring to the hitmanforhire website.

The court bubbled with barely suppressed giggles as he was questioned about why exactly he had chosen the number in his email address, judas69@gmail.com. It was just a number, he insisted, looking as amused as the rest of the room. But the hilarity was to be short lived. Buckley disappeared back to his life and matters in the court room turned to the technicalities of forensic computer examinations. The week ended with lists of computer data found on the reception computer in Downes & Howard. Finally this was the first tantalising glimpse at the full text of the emails that had promised so much in O'Connell's opening speech and an indication of just how much these particular nuggets would be mired in technical information. Each email would be read out in the order it was discovered. If it had been discovered cached on more than one computer, the email would be read once again for each discovery. The contents of the flirty emails between 'Lyingeyes' and 'Luciano' would become almost sickeningly familiar by the end of the trial.

But the computer evidence wasn't proof of much more than two people flirting under dubious circumstances without the ricin evidence. The courtroom went quiet as two army witnesses took the stand. Commandants P.J.

Butler and Peter Daly were from the Explosives Ordnance Division (EOD), and were called in when the news had arrived from America that Eid might have been harbouring deadly toxins in his prison cell. There was evidence of an evening swoop by men dressed in white sterile suits, the finding of the lens case and its subsequent testing and transport to the UK. A veil of secrecy surrounded the three scientists from the UK who had been responsible for the final confirmation of the presence of ricin. LGC Ltd had formerly been the laboratory of the Government Chemist, the court was told, until it succumbed to privatisation and became a commercial enterprise. The description of the precautions that had been taken with the little lens case lifted the story briefly out of farce and into the realms of James Bond.

There was one scientist to process the case and swab it out with sterile cotton buds to make the samples for testing, another scientist in a different lab carried out the test. Emma Stubberfield, the biologist who had tested the samples in a nearby veterinary lab, was called back to the stand to answer questions about her results, which showed a fail on one of the tests. This was normal scientific practice, she explained. It was necessary to show the average result because this kind of thing happened all the time. The results were produced and suddenly became another piece of evidence in the trial.

Both defence teams were unhappy that they had not been allowed to hire independent scientists to verify the results but Dr Stephen Kippen, the man in charge at LGC, explained that there was no guarantee that whatever ricin had been present would have been stable enough to have survived for over a year since the initial tests were carried out. There was no guarantee that once it was in solution it would even still be ricin after this amount of time, he told them. He said he was happy that the lens case had been submitted to the best tests available, and that there was no better test. He knew that because he was developing a better one himself and he hadn't perfected it yet, he said.

The trial dragged on. Four weeks … five … the first month passed without mention. The email evidence trickled into the record; countless emails between 'Tony Luciano' and 'Lying Eyes', who should not have kept referring to herself as Sharon. The emails were read out as they had been extracted from the four computers in the case: the Advent desktop from the reception in Downes & Howard, Robert Howard's Toshiba laptop, the Iridium laptop from Collins's home, and the merged hard drive that represented the two computers seized from Eid's Nevada home. The emails had been opened on different computers, and sometimes reopened and read again when the reader needed to check something. Each finding had to be read into evidence as the story of 'Lying Eyes' and 'Tony Luciano' was set out before the jury.

The story came with illustrations. Gardaí had found several photographs on the various hard drives that corresponded with shots discussed in the emails or presented by Eid to Robert Howard when he had made his house call to extract money. Every time a photograph was shown, those in the public gallery would crane their necks to make out the distant shapes. The jury and all members of the judiciary and Bar were given little red booklets of photographs. Eid would stretch with the rest, beaming as he saw his beloved yellow Corvette, and himself with his arm around his smiling daughter's shoulders. The legal teams bickered about whether Eid should be identified in the photographs, a bone of contention since Eid's team were denying all forms of identification in connection with 'Tony Luciano'. Eid listened carefully and watched as the photographs were passed between the barristers. He grinned while they argued that the grinning man wearing shades in the sports car was him, eventually settling on an uneasy legal compromise. The photographs would be admitted into evidence for the jury as showing an unidentified man. Each photograph was described in turn for the benefit of the stenographer. This was a man in a car, this was the same man with an unidentified younger woman. Eid leaned forward to see the shot of Aya again and beamed up at the jury.

'That's my daughter.'

There was a moment of silence as the proud father's words settled uneasily into the court record. Then came several snorts of laughter as the impact of what had been said sank in. Eid grinned all the wider and nodded vigorously before compounding his mistake.

'That's my daughter.'

Eid's defence team sat down and allowed the prosecution to continue. So the computer evidence dragged on. The callous details of the proposed murder were read again and again, never quite losing their emphasis. Collins and Eid sat impassively as the courtship that had been conducted between their computers was picked over in minute detail. Eid would grin as the more bizarre emails were read but Collins did not.

It can't have been the first time she and her sons had heard the details in the almost playful emails, but it was possibly only now the full implications were sinking in.

When the email detailing the allegations she made about P.J. Howard involving prostitutes and transvestites was read out, with its preamble of a cosy evening at home with her younger son, the blood drained from her face. The contents of this email showed that Collins was capable of saying anything in order to advance her own interests. The smear was a callous attack on the man who had shown her nothing but love.

The trial continued on its course as the summer term passed. Every Monday crowds of potential jurors gathered to be picked for the latest list of trials and a succession of men and women were brought in to be tried. But through all of this the proceedings in Court Two continued. The two defendants took their seats every morning and endured the scrutiny of the busy public gallery. Collins had worked her way through several Post It pads by now while Eid was busy making friends with everyone. He would joke with the prison guards and journalists, smiling a welcome as each familiar face arrived for the new day's business. After his gaffe with the photographs he seemed to have relaxed, listening to the day's evidence with a look of almost rapt attention. Collins was equally alert but seemed markedly less impressed; frequently bowing her head to murmur to her sons and shaking her head vigorously when the evidence seemed damning. By now attention had moved to what the conspirators had told the gardaí and statement after statement was read to the jury. It was slow going. Collins's defence team kept querying differences between the written account of the interview and a transcript of the video that had been taken of it. The gardaí were not trained stenographers it was pointed out. They did the best they could. But Collins had said she was unhappy with the way things were written down. Eventually a copy of the video of her interrogation was produced and the whole court could watch Collins from above as she patted and pleated her handkerchief.

The sound, never good on these video recordings, was terrible. The courtroom acoustics did not help. The reporters in the public benches leaned forward to hear better and even the jury showed their frustration from time to time. Two jurors had holidays booked in a week or so. Time was getting on. The taped interview was eventually abandoned and the prosecution case neared its end. But before it could do so the Court was to hear yet another extraordinary twist in an already unbelievable trial.

The only piece of evidence that gave Collins a partial alibi was given by John Keating, a builder from Limerick. He had changed the locks on the door of Downes & Howard after it had been burgled. But he had also met Collins on 16 August, the day she was supposed to have emailed and called 'Luciano.' Keating was cross examined on the stand on two occasions but gave reliable evidence. He said his own records showed he had been with Collins on this crucial date and produced evidence to support his story. His recollections of events, which he gave honestly, caused the prosecution to worry.

And so the trial entered its seventh week and neared its end. But Collins, for one, was not going down without a fight.

CHAPTER 14:

THE DEVIL IN THE RED DRESS

A defendant in a criminal trial does not have to give evidence. It is, after all, not up to them to prove their innocence. There had never been much doubt, however, that when the defendant was Sharon Collins, the defence would be lengthy and entertaining. When it actually began it even had the glitter of celebrity about it. There was a flurry of excitement on the morning of 1 July when those arriving into court across the Round Hall noticed the familiar figure of Gerry Ryan, the celebrated broadcaster, standing deep in conversation with Collins's legal team.

The question of his attendance had been hotly debated among the press benches since an email which Collins had sent to his show had been read out in the court earlier in the trial, on 17 June.

In the email to the *Gerry Ryan Show,* which is broadcast on RTE 2FM, Collins had accused Howard of having a fondness for kinky sex. Although the allegations were later refuted by P.J. Howard, her accusations had now entered the public domain.

According to the email, which was read out in court after it was retrieved from a computer, P.J. Howard was into swinging. He took full advantage of the more relaxed atmosphere in Spain and would bring her out to swinging parties on a regular basis, she wrote. She would agree to go but only to look, definitely not to touch, she wrote, adding that he would pester her day in, day out to sleep with strangers while he watched. She said she would rather let him go off and sleep with the transvestite hookers he liked to visit than get involved in any of that kind of thing. She further claimed this was the cause of the most regular arguments they had as a couple.

> 'I find myself in an unbearable situation, with very few real options and decided to share it with your listeners in the hope that hearing it on the air would clarify things for me and perhaps push me into making the move that frightened me so much.'

It continued.

> 'He has a holiday home abroad and likes us to spend as much time there as possible. However, the main attraction for him there is the sex industry—he uses prostitutes and transvestites regularly, but what he really wants is for me to engage in what he describes as "strange sex". It's never ending, he will wake me early in the morning or during the night asking me when I'm going to have sex with him or when will I have a threesome with a male escort and himself. He has even told me that he would love it if I would work as a prostitute and that this would really turn

him on. I find the idea beyond repulsive. He has insisted on many occasions that we go to Swingers' Clubs while abroad and has been unbearable to live with afterwards as I do not want to partake in what goes on there. I've witnessed things that I sincerely wish I never had to see. Don't get me wrong, I'm no prude, but I simply do not see myself this way.'

Gerry Ryan never received the email; it got lost in the mountain of correspondence his show received. Even though she tried to get the story aired a second time with a pitch entitled 'Sleeping with the enemy,' it was never read out on air. Ironically when the details of Collins's grievances finally did reach an audience, it was without her carefully placed anonymity intact.

She had always maintained that while she admitted writing the letter in a fit of pique against Howard one evening while she was in Spain, she had never actually hit send. The fact that her computer had received an automated response from the RTE server was something that was not explained to her satisfaction, so now Ryan himself had been summoned to court to explain what had happened. He ended up giving his evidence before the Prosecution had quite finished presenting their case.

It was explained to the court that he and his producer, Siobhán Hough, were about to catch a flight out of the country and would simply not be available to take the stand in a more conventional slot. Standing to swear to tell the truth, the whole truth and nothing but the truth, he looked every inch the successful broadcaster in a dark pin striped suit, his hair slicked back severely. The court went quiet as he sat down to give his evidence. It was well known that the trial had been discussed on his show and he had commented that he had never seen the letter in question. Michael Bowman, a barrister on Collins's defence team, had pointed out that this proved there was no evidence that the letter had ever been sent, backing up his client's version of events. There was a lot riding on this witness.

The evidence, as it was quickly run through, turned out to be something of an anticlimax. The show received about two thousand emails a month, Ryan said, only a fraction of them got to air. His production team went through all the emails and filtered the interesting ones out before giving them to him to read over. To the best of his knowledge, he had never received a letter giving the details Collins had written.

Hough took the stand next. She couldn't remember the letter either or the one that had been titled 'Sleeping with the enemy' the contents of which had disappeared without trace since being written. And that was it. Ryan left the courtroom followed by a gaggle of reporters hoping for a few extra words to pad out their copy. None was forthcoming and Ryan and his producer exited stage left to catch their plane.

The defence soon got underway properly. Collins's friends and family took the stand to paint her as a victim in the whole sordid affair. Her elder sisters appeared one after the other to insist that they had never stayed with Collins at Ballybeg House in 2006. Their evidence was over quickly and with a nod to their sister they were gone.

Now the waiting was almost over. While neither of the two accused were under any obligation whatsoever to take the stand themselves, it was hoped by the press that one or both of them would. Collins herself had been musing over lunch whether or not she should take the stand. Although not quite as chatty as her co-defendant, she had struck up conversations with some of the press. Anxious about her public image she asked this author, 'Should I give evidence?' The honest answer, the only one that wouldn't have been a bare faced lie was, 'We all want you to.'

She paused in the stairwell leading to the toilets, just off the Round Hall.

'They've been telling me I should but I wasn't sure. I think everyone would like to know what really happened though. Don't you?'

'Of course.'

There was only the briefest of pauses after the last of the witnesses left the stand before Collins stood up and made her way towards the witness box. There was an almost imperceptible intake of breath and those in the back seats leaned forward so as not to miss a word. Collins paid no attention. This was her moment and she was making the most of it. She sat down, her frame tiny against the dark wood of the judge's bench, and smiled at the jury. O'Higgins stood up and led her through an easy protestation of her innocence. It was only when he sat down and the Prosecution's barrister stood up that matters got interesting.

The barrister, Una Ní Raifeartaigh, was chosen to handle the cross examination for strategic reasons. It proved to be a prudent move as she had deftly navigated through the majority of the technical evidence and knew how to handle Collins. She was more than a match for Collins's charms and within moments, as the line was drawn in the sand between them, Collins's smile faltered for the first time. The first matter to be dealt with was the evidence from John Keating. Ní Raifeartaigh immediately raised 16 August with Collins.

Would Collins's mother remember her arriving at her house with a builder, the barrister asked.

Collins nodded emphatically.

'Yes, of course!'

But her mother was an elderly woman, after all. Collins smiled disarmingly.

'She wouldn't remember the date.'

When Ní Raifeartaigh probed Collins about her own recollection, she declared it to be rock solid.

'I have been thinking back for quite a long time,' Collins said.

The barrister reminded Collins that she only got the evidence about the 16 August emails in May, just before the trial started. It had taken the gardaí quite some time to decode what they found on the numerous hard drives. When Ní Raifeartaigh asked if Collins suddenly remembered that morning with Keating, two years later, she was met with a short 'Yes.'

A change in tack, the subject moved to the rest of Collins's alibi.

Ní Raifeartaigh asked her if she had told her partner that she was being blackmailed. Collins smiled wryly. Of course she hadn't, not considering what the blackmail had been about. Ní Raifeartaigh pushed further, asking if she had told him about Maria Marconi at all. Collins shook her head. She said that she had wanted to find out if she could write first, and then surprise Howard with the news when she had something to show him. She retorted that it wasn't unusual not to tell him something like that.

'People keep things to themselves and don't tell their partners all the time,' said Collins.

Ní Raifeartaigh put it to Collins that she probably needed the time to get her story straight. She had been well practised by the time she started telling people about Marconi, the barrister remarked.

For the first time, irritation showed in Collins. 'It wasn't difficult to tell them what happened. It's easy to tell a story when you know what you have done.'

So these seventy phone calls between her phone and Essam Eid's phone, was she claiming she had made 70 calls to a blackmailer? asked Ní Raifeartaigh.

Collins shook her head again. No, some of them were to Maria Marconi.

But they're all to the same numbers, Ní Raifeartaigh countered.

The numbers were withheld. It was difficult to tell, said Collins.

The barrister asked her about the emails.

Collins responded that it was easy; she wasn't Lying Eyes.

When Ní Raifeartaigh highlighted that Lying Eyes kept signing herself Sharon and she used Collins's mother's maiden name when she applied for a job with hitmanforhire.net, Collins kept her answers simple.

'That wasn't me. I don't have any firearms experience.'

'I'm glad you pointed that out,' retorted the barrister.

Collins insisted she wasn't Lying Eyes. 'I suppose you could say that it's your job to bring in a guilty verdict but I am not Lying Eyes.'

But the name is so appropriate.

'Is it?' Collins smiled politely. 'I wouldn't know.'

'Didn't you listen to any music in the 70s?'

Collins nodded. She knew the song but only after a friend of hers had phoned her and sang her the chorus. Ní Raifeartaigh was unimpressed.

'Do you know it's about a young beautiful woman moving in with an older man and cheating on him?'

'I just heard the first verse,' retorted Collins.

It was a very popular song in its day. You must know it. Ní Raifeartaigh pointed out they were both of an age and should share the same popular culture.

'Robert is into old music. I am actually into Justin Timberlake.'

Collins laughed and fluttered her eyelashes toward the jury. She had not written those emails.

But they had so much detail in them; detail that only Collins could know, the barrister remarked.

Collins stood firm and said she hadn't written them.

Ní Raifeartaigh didn't let up. She put it to Collins that she had used the name Bernie Lyons to sign up for the Lying Eyes address.

Collins said she hadn't.

The barrister wasn't put out by Collins's continued denials, and put it to her that she had identified herself as the 'devil in the red dress' to the man she was hiring to kill her partner and his sons.

She had done no such thing. She would never call herself a devil. She was a religious woman, Collins added. 'I just find it amazing that somebody would identify themselves like that to a would-be assassin.'

She smiled at the jury again, saying that she was totally innocent. She said she had made all this clear to the gardaí when they had questioned her but they hadn't taken everything down.

Ní Raifeartaigh acknowledged that Collins was not happy with the interviews.

Collins nodded, all serious. The accused had a long list of points she had wanted her defence to bring up about them but, and she turned a 100 watt smile back towards the jury, 'I think there are people who want to get away so for the sake of finishing up.'

The barrister was not impressed by this grandstanding. The jury would have the right to request the videos if they wanted them once they had begun their deliberations and it was up to them to decide if the differences mattered. But right now it was the emails from Lying Eyes that interested the prosecutor.

Collins was insistent. She wasn't Lying Eyes. She was a victim, she had been blackmailed. She had never made any secret about the €15,000 payment to Teresa Engle.

'I think the position I find myself in is ludicrous,' Collins declared.

'It's of your own making, Ms Collins.'

'I wouldn't agree with that.'

She denied giving the tracking number to anyone apart from the blackmailer.

The barrister asked how Eid got hold of it.

Someone else might have had it, Collins told her and said that she certainly hadn't used the Iridium laptop to check the tracking number herself.

But someone went onto the FedEx page with that tracking number at 8.10 a.m. on 16 August. Ní Raifeartaigh asked Collins if she noticed anyone using her computer at home when she went down to make her coffee?

When the barrister asked Collins to look at the evidence, Ní Raifeartaigh pointed out that it would have had to be someone with a particularly Machiavellian mind to set her up. They would have had to sneak around her house to use the computer and when they were framing her as a femme fatale, they would have had to be so precise as to do internet searches for diet pills and flights to Malaga while they were looking for a hitman. Whoever had set her up must have known her very well, the barrister added.

Piece by piece, the internet evidence was brought out and pored over. If it hadn't been Collins, who did she suggest it was, Ní Raifeartaigh asked her. The barrister pointed out that there were a limited number of people who had access to all the computers that the emails had been sent from. There was Collins; the others would all appear to be the Howards but they were the very people the plot had sought to kill. She asked who Collins would suggest had written the emails if it wasn't her?

Collins appeared to lose her composure for the first time in the trial.

'I have been brought down to the garda station. I have been questioned at length. I have been charged with crimes I most certainly did not commit. I have been put into prison; you can't imagine the effect that has had on my life. I am not going to accuse anybody of anything when I don't know,' she said.

The accused said that the trial had had a major impact on her family, and she was serious as she agreed that her sisters had used the Irish versions of their names to give evidence. She said it was a hugely embarrassing situation for everyone.

'It has destroyed my life and my children's lives.'

Ní Raifeartaigh dragged the attention away from Collins to the emails' proposed victims, P.J. Howard and his two sons. The situation was surely more humiliating for Howard.

'You were a couple for how long? Eight years?'

'It's ten years now.'

For the first time Collins gave a definite indication to the question that had been buzzing around the courtroom since P.J. Howard had kissed her as he left, and would continue to buzz long after the trial was over. In her eyes anyway, they were still an item. Collins's eyes widened as she spoke of his unwavering support.

'I know that if I was shown the amount of evidence P.J. has been shown of someone trying to kill my children I wouldn't let my heart get in my way.'

Then she said she was angry about the Gerry Ryan email being read out in court. Even though P.J. Howard hadn't been in court that day, he had been in the country, he had read the papers and seen the headlines. Ní Raifeartaigh nodded.

'He was a man with a secret.'

'Yes.'

'You let that secret out of the bag.'

Collins was indignant. This was one mess that was not down to her.

'I didn't let the secret out of the bag. If that letter had been aired on the Gerry Ryan Show it would have been done as an anonymous letter,' said Collins.

Collins then accepted that the email had been sent, she hadn't realised it had but if there had been email confirmation …

'Nevertheless though it was an anonymous and private matter,' she retorted and went on to say that the letter should never have been read out in court. On top of that, she said the copy that the gardaí had recovered was incomplete. If they could have seen the whole letter they would have seen how many nice things she had written about P.J. Howard as well.

The prosecutor asked if she could assume from Collins's remarks that the contents were true.

'It certainly was a thing that P.J. and I had discussed … It was part of what we had discussed,' Collins responded.

'Was it true?'

'Some of it was—various bits but a lot of that letter wasn't retrieved.'

It didn't give a full picture, Collins complained.

Ní Raifeartaigh asked her if she stood by the things she had written about Howard.

'I don't think I need to explain the private matters that go on between two people,' Collins responded.

Ní Raifeartaigh wasn't about to give up any time soon. She pointed out the obvious. The way the allegations had also turned up in the emails between 'Lying Eyes' and 'Tony Luciano', almost as if they were a motive. Collins shook her head vigorously.

'It's absolutely not a motive to kill three people.'

But it was a motive for blackmail, argued the prosecutor, even though the sky hadn't fallen since the matter had been aired in court. She asked if they were true. Had he asked Collins to sleep with other men?

'It was discussed. I'm not sure how serious he was about it,' said Collins.

'He made the suggestion to you?'

'It was discussed.'

And the transvestites?

'Yes.'

'How did you feel?'

'I most certainly didn't like it … as I've said, after that it was no longer an issue. Well it wasn't mentioned again.'

Ní Raifeartaigh was not convinced. It just went away?

Collins nodded, smiling again.

She explained that there had been rows about certain things and she had been very angry at the time. That's when she had written everything down. Including the email she had sent to Marconi that she had subsequently been blackmailed with. But it hadn't been discussed after that row. It might have been because they were travelling but it was certainly never discussed. She said that she didn't want to discuss the matter now.

But Ní Raifeartaigh insisted that it was relevant. This was a conspiracy to murder trial and for that you needed a motive. It was far easier to order the killing of someone you hated and that's what the emails would seem to suggest, argued Ní Raifeartaigh.

Collins was shaking her head again, a concerned frown pitting her brow.

'I know you need a motive to kill somebody but that sort of thing is a motive to leave somebody. It isn't a motive to kill somebody. I most certainly didn't hate P.J.,' said Collins.

The barrister shook her head; that wasn't the only motive. Ní Raifeartaigh put it to her that money was the major motive to hire someone to kill the Howards.

Collins leaned forward as she shook her head. That was ridiculous. P.J. had always promised to look after her if the relationship ended one day.

'P.J. had always told me that if the relationship didn't work out he would look after me very well. If I said to P.J. it has run its course and I'm leaving he would look after me very well. He always made it absolutely clear to me and I believed him.'

She told the court she wouldn't have needed to kill P.J. Howard to be sure of a home and an income.

But the barrister wasn't letting it go. If P.J. Howard had been so intent on looking after her, then why hadn't he said anything to his solicitor, Ní Raifeartaigh asked. He had everything else in writing.

This was indeed a problem. Collins tried her best to explain the situation. She said that P.J. had been in the process of setting something up but he hadn't got round to it. It was just one of those things but it didn't mean that he wouldn't have done it.

The barrister then said that P.J. Howard wouldn't marry Collins.

But he had wanted to, Collins responded. She said he made that very clear.

Ní Raifeartaigh put it to her that it must have been humiliating, him refusing to get married.

'I never made a secret of the fact I wanted to get married,' said Collins.

And there was a wedding reception where 39 people didn't know that the bride and groom had not actually got married. Not to mention the proxy marriage itself, added Ní Raifeartaigh, who had done an excellent cross examination.

Collins was on the stand for two days of cross examination. As everyone gathered for her second day of evidence she looked tense. Her face was drawn with the tiredness showing under her eyes. She suddenly looked markedly older than her legal opponent as she once again took the stand and Ní Raifeartaigh stood up to continue the questioning. The drill on this second day was to be a detailed re-examination of the computer evidence. Once again the barrister pointed out that it would have taken someone extremely devious to set her up.

'Either it's you or it's someone setting you up by immediately doing the kind of searches and interests that you have, then going into Lying Eyes.'

'It's not me anyway,' Collins told her.

Ní Raifeartaigh pointed out how the person had known her so well. There was the order for Reductil, the searches for weight loss tips. 'Tesco Diets is an odd place to go to if you are a mystery man setting you up for conspiracy for murder,' the barrister said.

She pointed out that Collins was known for her get rich quick schemes. This latest scheme to murder the Howards was simply more of the same. Ní Raifeartaigh started reading out the Lying Eyes emails. She asked Collins if she thought the language sounded like the kind of thing Collins would have written herself. Collins was adamant she had not written those terrible emails.

'I will never get over the shock of this but I certainly did not write that. It's terrible!'

So was she suggesting that Niall or Robert Howard wrote the emails instead? They would be the only ones in a position to use all the laptops, stated the barrister.

'I didn't suggest that. The only thing I am suggesting here is that I didn't do this. I would never do this,' Collins responded.

Collins's calm veneer was wearing decidedly thin. Ní Raifeartaigh pushed on. She asked where the emails were that would back up her story of blackmail?

Collins was quick with her reply. She had written those from an internet café in Spain and then her email inbox had been wiped. She added that she had assumed the gardaí would be able to get the emails from Eircom. She said that she was telling the truth, that she would never do anything to harm Howard and his sons.

'I had a really, really good relationship with P.J.'s sons. They were like sons to me. I tried to be like a mother to them,' she said for good measure.

Collins insisted that she had not written those emails with all the horrible things in them. She continued with the line that she must have been set up. She said she hadn't even known where the laptop in Ballybeg House was, that it had disappeared after a party the boys had had.

Each answer that Collins gave was a lie. She could not answer any questions because she could not tell the truth. The details were causing her problems.

She kept on saying that the Iridium laptop was not in the house, even though it had been located at Ballybeg House, and the dial-ups from the house exactly matched the timing of the emails sent from the Lying Eyes account.

In spite of the weight of the evidence stacked against her, Collins continued to deny the truth.

'The Iridium wasn't there.'

But the barrister wasn't letting it go.

The barrister said that there had been contact between Lying Eyes and 'Luciano' on the night of 15 August, and then again the following morning at about 8am.

'Did you notice a blackmailer walking around your house at 8.10 a.m. that morning?' Ní Raifeartaigh asked.

The user had also accessed FedEx with a tracking number that only Collins had. There were also the phone calls, phone calls that had even followed her to Spain when she had travelled there, Ní Raifeartaigh reminded her.

Collins was quickly losing her composure. She was the victim of blackmail, she claimed; not a would-be murderer.

'What happened to me was a terrifying, frightening thing and what you are talking about is a terrifying, alarming thing.'

By now she was getting visibly upset. Her opponent pressed her further and asked if she knew who set her up.

'The mystery person could be Robert Howard,' Ní Raifeartaigh suggested.

Collins was indignant.

'I never said that. I was mad about those boys.'

Finally Collins broke down, the tears streaming down her cheeks as she dabbed at them with a handkerchief proffered by the stenographer. She knew what had happened to her, or so she said. She had explained it so many times, but she could not say who set her up.

'I am sitting down here accused of the most horrendous crimes. Accused of trying to hurt people that I care about, that I had relationships with, things that I did not do!'

By now the tears were coming unchecked.

'I did foolish things, I did stupid things. I shouldn't have written that letter about P.J. but I certainly didn't plot to kill anybody,' she said crying.

Ní Raifeartaigh appeared unimpressed by the tears.

'You got in here to try and do what you always do, and you sit there, trying to manipulate the jury, smiling at the jury.'

'I'm not smiling at the jury,' Collins replied.

Ní Raifeartaigh reminded her that she had been the day before.

'Sometimes when I'm nervous I smile. I'm not trying to manipulate, I'm telling the truth. I have always, always told the truth on this. I am not here to manipulate anybody,' said Collins.

The barrister listened attentively and said that Collins had repeatedly tried to manipulate, why else would she have written those three pleading letters to the Director of Public Prosecutions?

Collins sat in the witness box looking broken, the tears still falling, her eyes red with crying. She tried one last time to state her case.

'I was out of my home, my family in bits. I was absolutely shattered. I wasn't trying to manipulate, I was trying to explain the damage this case is having to my family.'

Finally her cross-examination was over. She stepped out of the witness box and returned to her sons. Gary put a protective arm around his mother's shoulders and she turned her face into him for a moment. Her defence case was almost over and her evidence had not been the triumphant opportunity to put her story across one final time that she had hoped for. The prosecution had seen to that.

Attention now turned to Eid, who had been sitting watching his co-accused's cross examination with interest. He had wanted to take the stand himself but decided against doing so.

All that was left was the closing speeches. Robert and Niall Howard reappeared to see the case come to a close, their appearance causing a small ripple of interest among the public benches as Ní Raifeartaigh once again took to her feet to close the prosecution case.

This had been an 'extraordinary and bizarre trial' she told the jury. She warned that the case had been too easily dismissed by the media as trivial, simply because no-one had died.

'From a distance this may look like a cheap thriller that Sharon Collins herself may have written but this is a tragedy for everyone involved,' the barrister said.

She warned that it would be wrong to dismiss this case as trivial; the finding of ricin in Eid's cell lifted the matter out of 'fantasy and speculation'.

She urged the jury to look beneath the farcical elements to the darker truth beneath because, 'treachery lies in honeyed words'. She warned that while the jury may feel they were dealing with fools, they were dangerous fools. The case against the two defendants was strong but the smoking gun, where Sharon Collins was concerned, was the fact that someone had checked the tracking number of the parcel sent to Essam Eid's address at 8.10 a.m. on the morning of 16 August from Ballybeg House. It was the one thing that Collins could not talk her way out of, though she might 'talk and talk and talk'.

The defence counsel, Michael Bowman made the final speech in Collins's defence. He pointed out to the jury that they could not discount John Keating's evidence, which gave Collins a partial alibi on 16 August, a day the prosecution put so much emphasis on. He pointed out the discrepancies in the notes of the interviews Collins had given to the gardaí compared with the video evidence. He impressed upon them the possibility that someone else had written the emails; that Collins's story of Maria Marconi was the truth and she herself had been a victim of blackmail. He also drew their attention to the ricin evidence. The fact that the lens case had not been listed in Eid's personal belongings at his arrest and the failure of tests at both stages of analysis, both a field test and at the veterinary lab in the UK, was something they should definitely bear in mind.

He warned the jury against slavishly following computer generated evidence. He sat down, to allow Eid's team to argue their case.

Of the three arguments, Eid's was the only one delivered by his senior counsel. David Sutton took to his feet and spoke to the jury. His client was the 'patsy' in all of this. The jury should be under no illusions that it was Sharon Collins who was the 'great white defendant' while Eid was simply the 'patsy being dragged along in the wake'.

The case against Eid, he said was not Dial M for Murder, it was clearly a case of Dial M for Money.

'It was a clownish operation by clowns in the hope of hooking fools.'

He dismissed the ricin evidence out of hand. The only evidence before the jury was that Eid was in possession of an empty contact lens case in Limerick Prison. Despite what the State may have suggested the jury was not to assume that Eid had any contact with ricin before he left the States.

'There is no such evidence before you and the State reporting that Mr Eid was making it does not make it so,' he said.

The same was true of the computer evidence, he told the jury. Eid was by no means the only person who had access to the phones and computers seized from Camden Cove Street. He reminded them that the only person who had come before them with a criminal record was Teresa Engle, someone who had a vested interest to give damning evidence against Eid and someone whose word should not be trusted but he reminded them that the charges Engle had faced in the States had been over a case of extortion, not conspiracy to murder. The scheme was clumsy and foolish with an 'asinine plot worthy of the Cohen brothers.' He implored the jury to treat Eid with justice and discretion and not be swayed by the grand accusations of the Prosecution.

As Sutton sat back down, all that was left was for the jury to be charged to begin their deliberations. On 7 July 2008 the eight men and four women began their deliberations. It would be another two days before Sharon Collins and Essam Eid learned their fate and even longer before they would discover what price they would pay.

CHAPTER 15:

THE HOUSE ALWAYS WINS

After the verdict was read out the court emptied in quick fashion. The press hurried round to the front of the building to wait for the statements that would inevitably follow. P.J. Howard's statement had already arrived, emailed to the waiting press within minutes of the jury's decision, the Howard family now showing a united front and pleading for a privacy that was unlikely to follow until P.J. Howard had dropped his torch for the 'devil in the red dress'. Short and succinct it intended to draw a line under the whole sorry mess.

'We are relieved that this long trial has come to a conclusion and we would like to express our appreciation to the members of the jury for their patience and attention. It is also appropriate to record our gratitude to the many people who have assisted us during this difficult period. We now look forward to getting on with our lives and we request the privacy that's necessary to assist us in this respect. It is not our intention to make any further statement.'

But the media still hung around. Word soon went round that Collins's solicitor Eugene O'Kelly planned to make a statement to the press. A few minutes later, after a large crowd had assembled, microphones and flashguns at the ready, O'Kelly took his place, flanked by Gary and David, their father Noel a reassuring presence at their shoulder. The crowd surged forward but the statement, when it came, was little more than a holding pattern.

'Sharon Collins has maintained her innocence in this trial. The jury have found her guilty. The judge has adjourned sentencing for the preparation of reports. Accordingly, in relation to the comment, it would be inappropriate to comment any further on the verdict at this stage,' he said.

The outstretched arms of the media remained thrust forward as he turned his attention to the rest of the Collins family.

'The two persons most affected other than Sharon as a result of this verdict are her two sons. These are two fine young men who have displayed loyalty, devotion and love to there mother. They have stood by her in this trial and their lives have now been shattered as a result of the outcome.'

The journalists were asked to steer clear of the boys for the time being and give them time to adjust to the 'changed circumstances'.

'These circumstances are entirely not of their making and they now have to move on,' the solicitor added.

O'Kelly refused to be drawn on the matter of an appeal. The sentences hadn't been handed down yet, he reminded the assembled journalists. There would be time enough for that at the sentence in the autumn.

And that was it. The Collins family hurried off to grieve their loss while Sharon was led away in handcuffs, her face red with shock as the cold metal of the cuffs brought home the reality of her situation. She had lost the case, and she would have to wait three months to discover what the punishment would be. All she could do now was try to make the most of her situation. She was to wait for her sentence in the Dochas Centre, the women's wing of Mountjoy Prison, home to some of Ireland's most notorious female criminals.

In prison she was visited by her sons, and P.J. Howard also visited at the jail.

Despite everything that had been said in court, and the final conclusion made by the jury, P.J. Howard was determined to show his continuing support to the woman who had betrayed him so bitterly. He still refused to accept a word that had been said against Collins in court and worked feverishly behind the scenes trying to help her in any way he could.

The press interest in Collins's failed plot didn't diminish. She had become one of the elite group of detainees that continue to make the headlines even when they're doing nothing. As soon as she arrived in the Dochas Centre the stories started. 'Prison services insiders' provided stories of the tears that greeted the beginning of her incarceration. Then came the stories that she was picky when it came to prison food. Collins, famous for her purchase of Reductil on the internet, was reluctant to eat the stodgy prison fare, it was claimed. She had insisted on a list of dietary requirements, which it was reported with some glee, were refused. Every suggestion that the millionaire's ex was getting no special treatment was seized on and treated to a front page splash in the tabloids. The public were treated to a dissection of the menus she would be served with and the company she would now be keeping, a world away from Ennis's ladies who lunch.

The CVs of her fellow inmates were trotted out again and again. There were the Mulhall sisters, passed into Dublin history as the Scissor Sisters after they chopped up the body of their mother's boyfriend to dispose of it. But most illustrious among the inhabitants of Mountjoy's women's prison was the Black Widow herself, Catherine Nevin, who had been convicted of murdering her husband, a natural ally given the circumstances. No one was particularly surprised when the stories started being circulated that Collins and the Black Widow had forged a bond. It was logical, after all Nevin had gone through everything Collins was now facing, and there was talk of her mounting an appeal. Who better to offer hope to the broken Lying Eyes?

But Nevin wasn't Collins's only friend. Not content with paying his respects, P.J. Howard continued to try and clear her name. He hired numerous private detectives, to search for Marconi, Collins's elusive writing teacher and alibi.

P.J. Howard wasn't deterred. He clung to the idea that Collins was still the innocent women he had courted so passionately a decade ago. He had no hidden agenda, he said, 'other than the fact I would like to see Sharon free.'

Many court observers wondered why he was remaining loyal to Collins, sticking with such a duplicitous femme fatale, but P.J. Howard was determined. Throughout the summer his faith in her never weakened and speculation started to mount that he would himself take the stand in her defence when the sentencing finally came round. From her cell in the Dochas Centre, Collins took hope from both P.J. Howard's faith and in her own chances of a successful appeal. By the time the courts were back in session and it was time to once again go to the Four Courts to learn when her sentence would finally be handed down, she was upbeat.

The prison food might have hung a few more pounds on her previously skinny frame and her hair suffered from the lack of a regular cut and blow dry but Collins was in high spirits as she sat in her old familiar haunt under the stairs on Wednesday, 8 October, in the first week of the new court year. As she waited once again for her sons to arrive to join her in court, she chatted animatedly to the prison officer who stood at her side. It was almost an end to waiting and Collins was her usual bubbly, expressive self. Her hands fluttered in front of her chest as she talked, punctuating her words. Her faith in her own innocence was as strong as ever as she asked for an analysis of her trial. She was still having difficulty believing that the jury could have thought she was guilty but she presented herself with her head held high and her best foot forward. She greeted her son David with a dazzling smile, which was also turned towards her legal team as they went into a last minute huddle outside the courts. Her appearance was a mere formality. The real tension wouldn't hit until a month later.

Her co-accused was in equally good form. As always on his court appearances, Eid was laughing and joking with the prison guards, greeting them as old friends after a long absence. He had been in prison for over two years by now and any sentence he finally received would begin with that time taken off it. There was even speculation that he would have served his entire sentence if a sufficiently lenient jail term was handed down. But this court appearance was a brief affair, although as with any appearance of Lying Eyes and the man who had introduced himself as Tony Luciano, the media had turned out in force.

In court the defence teams were told that the long awaited sentences would be handed down in a month, on Monday, 3 November.

When that day finally dawned there was a heightened sense of anticipation. There had been feverish speculation over the weekend that P.J. Howard would be attending to hear his partner's fate. Court Two filled up early that morning as the interest levels peaked. Long before proceedings were due to start the public benches were being filled by the sombre suited figures of the barristers who did not have a prior engagement. The public posse was out in droves as well. Gathering early to secure a decent view they huddled in their seats and the regulars waved to each other like old friends before settling in for the main event. The press, of course, were out in force, for this was an end to one of the biggest stories of the year. For once, neither accused was anywhere to be seen.

Robert and Niall Howard had settled themselves on a bench outside the courtroom before entering. Many of those assembled felt for the two men. They had been dragged into a mess that was not of their own making. They were innocent victims of a ruthless extortionist and Collins. Finally Collins's supporters marched into view.

Her two sons walked in flanking the tiny frail figure of their grandmother, Bernadette, Collins's mother, who had been absent for much of the trial but was now here to support her daughter. They were also accompanied by their father Noel.

When the family party reached the courtroom it was to find Collins already in place, a female prison officer in the spot where one of her sons would have been before her conviction. She had lost the extra pounds that had caused much comment at her appearance a month previously and her hair was neatly styled. The black trouser suit was back with a mauve blouse just visible under the jacket. Her face was free of makeup and she looked serious as she greeted her mother and her sons. As the family took their seats, the prison officer kept her place, a human buffer to remind those gathered of the changed circumstances.

Eid for once was last to take his place. Dressed now for a cold Irish autumn, he wore a brown jumper with thin horizontal stripes under which, in accidental co-ordination with his co-accused, he wore a lilac shirt. Gone were the jeans in honour of the seriousness of the occasion and for once he too wore a black suit. But apart from the change in outfit his demeanour had not changed, and he smiled at familiar faces as he waited along with the rest for the trial to begin.

Suddenly a ripple of excitement went round the room. P.J. Howard had been seen crossing the Round Hall. He came in clutching a brown manila folder accompanied by a solicitor. The news slowly crept through the press benches that he had arrived with his own legal team and was intending to make a plea for clemency for the woman he had never stopped believing in. However, the Prosecution was unhappy. Prosecuting counsel Tom O'Connell told Justice Murphy that what P.J. Howard had prepared wasn't so much a victim impact statement, which as a victim he was fully entitled to give, but more a character reference more suited for the defence.

It was against this backdrop that the court began hearing more evidence. Superintendent John Scanlan took the stand to run through the familiar facts and informed the court that neither of the accused had ever come to the attention of the law before. O'Connell then outlined the sentences that had been imposed on similar cases in the past. The legislation had not been changed since the 19th Century, he said, and similar cases were few on the ground, but a sample of those that had passed through the courts in recent years tended to receive sentences around the seven year mark out of a maximum of ten. O'Connell pointed out that unlike the cases he had mentioned, Collins had aimed to kill three people and so should be looking at consecutive terms for each.

Then, underlining the way a victim impact statement would more normally sound, O'Connell read from a prepared statement from P.J. Howard's sons Robert and Niall. It was a brief document but direct. They had not suffered any loss of earning or physical injuries, they had written, but their lives were changed for ever.

'The incident has caused significant changes in our lives. The notion that we were made the subject of a contract to kill has affected us socially and emotionally. The degree of planning and the nature of the contract and the person by whom the contract was initiated, particularly in light of her relationship with our father, has exasperated the situation for us. As the injured parties we have become more self conscious and are now constantly looking over our shoulders and are ill at ease. The crime has impacted on our respective social and business lives. We are not as confident as we were and we feel that the respect that had existed among our peers in our business dealings is not the same as it used to be. Furthermore we believe the incident has weakened the quality of our relationship with our father.'

They summed up their situation for the Court.

'We cannot understand how we were propelled from our normal daily lives into such a national drama and shudder at the realisation that had the plan been effected we could have been poisoned to death. We believe it will take a long time, if at all, before we can put the incident behind us.'

So the sentence hearing crawled into the afternoon and still P.J. Howard had not taken the stand. The public gallery was full when the judge returned at 2.15 p.m. that afternoon. The numbers had swelled since the morning as the lunchtime news had announced the possibility of yet another twist in an extraordinary tale. Finally P.J. Howard was allowed to get up and say his piece, but with the proviso that he would simply read his statement and not stray into defence territory through cross examination. In a voice trembling with emotion, clutching the paper of the statement and a bottle of water, P.J. Howard made his plea. First he criticised the gardaí before turning his attention to the subject of the infamous Gerry Ryan letter.

'I would like to take this opportunity to refute the allegations made against me in the Court case and I wish to deny any and all of the allegations. I have never seen nor was I told by the Gardaí about an email that was supposedly sent to the Gerry Ryan Show,' he said.

Honour and reputation defended he turned his attention to the main purpose of his appearance.

'I have known Sharon Collins for approximately 9 years. During that time she had made a good home for us all and we were extremely happy together and got on very well. Sharon has a very positive outlook on life and she was very loving and giving of her time to our extended families. Sharon always kept an even keel and I have never known her to do anything drastic over those years. She is a very straightforward and honest person and if she wanted anything she would ask.

'Sharon is in my opinion one of the nicest people you could ever have been fortunate to know. She is a caring, loving and decent lady,' he said.

Collins cried as he spoke, extolling her virtues. He wanted the woman he loved to avoid jail and spread his cards on the table with a claim that raised eyebrows around the Court.

'I will not give up on Sharon and would have no hesitation whatsoever in living with her again.'

He had never been afraid of Collins, he said, and did not feel she would ever be a threat to his sons. Then, just as Collins had written to the Director of Public Prosecution, he made his own plea for the casualties who would form the collateral damage of the trial. Her mother and her sons had suffered enough since her conviction and he himself was feeling the strain.

'This is an extremely stressful situation for me and the prospect of Sharon being in prison for a long time is adding to this stress. Sharon has for many years overseen the dispensing of my medication and has been of great assistance to me in this regard. I have had no fear and still have no fear of her doing this,' he said.

Collins stared up at him and he had the court room's rapt attention as he finished his plea.

'In the circumstances I would urge the Court to take into account that Sharon has never been before the Courts in these circumstances previously and it is my view that she will never so appear again. I am urging the Court not to impose a custodial sentence.'

In a brief cross examination by O'Connell, P.J. Howard criticised what he perceived to be an attempt by the authorities to leave him, as Collins's supporter, out in the cold. He told Justice Murphy that the gardaí had never asked him to produce a statement and he had only found out his sons were doing so when they told him themselves. He said that he had 'waited and waited' before taking the decision to hire his own counsel. He got down out of the witness stand as Detective Sergeant Michael Moloney headed towards it to answer the allegations.

In an extraordinary display of frayed temper, P.J. Howard's animosity towards the gardaí was clear as he leaned his face toward DS Moloney and muttered through gritted teeth 'don't lie' before taking his seat.

DS Moloney, who was a very respected officer, was adamant though that Howard had been well aware he had the right to submit a statement and said that the matter had even been mentioned in passing, although he himself could not recall specifically inviting Howard to contribute. As DS Moloney gave his evidence, P.J. Howard could be seen shaking his head angrily.

P.J. Howard wasn't the only voice to wade in on Collins's behalf. Once her defence counsel stood up to put forward the mitigating factors, there was a litany of praise for the woman now known as 'the Devil in the Red Dress'.

Her former husband, Noel Collins, took the stand to paint a favourable picture of his ex-wife. Collins lived for her sons, he told the Court, and had never forced him to stick to the visiting times set down in their separation agreement. He could see his family whenever he wanted and she had never been anything other than a brilliant mother. He spoke of her dedication to her elderly mother and described Bernadette Coote's decline since her daughter's incarceration. She had once been the life and soul of the party, he said, a lady who liked to dance, but all that had left her under the weight of the embarrassment and public scrutiny. The whole affair had had a 'massive effect' on the family he said, 'friends, family, you just cast the net out.' As he went back to the body of the Court he crossed to where P.J. Howard was sitting, stopping to shake his hand in solidarity.

The Mayor of Ennis and the Bishop of Killaloe added their combined weight to the argument. Peter Considine, the Mayor, admitted he did not know Collins but was an old acquaintance of her mother. He argued that Bernadette Coote had been a particular victim of the affair. She now had to be brought to the supermarket late at night to avoid the hungry stares of the gossips. Even collecting her pension had become an obstacle course as she tried to avoid other customers in the Post Office, not going in if it was busy. Her health had deteriorated drastically and he echoed Noel Collins in his assessment that Mrs Coote was a mere shadow of her former self. Bishop Willie Walsh described Collins as 'an open, truthful, caring person' who deserved the mercy of the Court.

Consultant psychologist Brian Glanville, who had visited Collins on two occasions in the Dochas Centre, told the Court he had conducted psychometric personality tests on her and found Collins to have 'a passive, detached but dependent personality'. This could lead to conflicts in relationships, he said, making her feel trapped even while she craved security. He said that Collins had felt isolated in prison. She did not have much in common with her fellow inmates and didn't like the media spotlight that had been trained on her since the trial began. Collins felt that she was constantly being watched and the press scrutiny encouraged others to invade her privacy and eavesdrop on intimate conversations that then found their way into the next day's papers.

Several other family friends added their views to the pot, agreeing that Collins was a model mother and a lovely person. Even the chaplain and assistant governor of Mountjoy Women's prison had been asked to provide reports. Prisoner 46671 was 'a good worker' and 'a model prisoner' they said in efficiently brief reports. Collins's defence barrister, Paul O'Higgins, put forward a strong body of support for his client who sat closer to Eid than she ever had done during her trial, her face pink and blotchy as her fate came ever closer.

Now it was the turn of Eid's defence team to make their stand but there was no-one waiting in the wings to sing the praises of the poker dealer. He had lost everything, David Sutton told the judge. His house was gone; his job lost forever; even both his wives had jumped ship. Sutton painted the picture of a lonely, broken man, at odds with the outwardly relaxed figure who had appeared to doze as the evidence was run through one last time. Just turned 53, Eid was not in good health. He had suffered heart attacks in the past and had a pace-maker which needed medical supervision. He also suffered from non-insulin dependent diabetes that again required careful monitoring. Sutton described a man far away from home who spent most of his time in his solitary cell, playing solitaire with the cards that had once held full houses. Once again Eid was playing second fiddle in the Irish courts, his defence was brief and bar a couple of medical reports there were no voices raised in his support.

Eventually at almost four o'clock, all the facts had been laid out and the best foot put forward by the two defence teams. Justice Murphy rose to briefly consider his sentence while the court hummed in muted speculation. Finally it was time for Collins to stand to hear her fate. She stood facing the bench, one hand nervously playing with the middle button of her jacket, which she held protectively closed over her stomach. There was barely a flicker of emotion as she learnt that she would be spending the next six years in jail but at least she had been spared the threat of a consecutive sentence, all six of her convictions would be served out simultaneously. She sat down heavily and was hugged, once again, by younger son David.

Then it was the turn of Eid. The poker dealer wasn't smiling as he stood up to learn his punishment. The maximum sentence for extortion was fourteen years and he had already heard that his demands with a threat of death were considered serious by the Court. The DPP withdrew the three charges of conspiracy to murder against him, pronouncing the three *nolle prosequi*, but he could still come out with a higher sentence than the 'devil in the red dress'. In the end there was a parity of sorts as Eid was also handed a six year sentence. He also received a year each for the two charges of handling stolen goods from the robbery at Downes & Howard but all three of his sentences were to run side by side, meaning that, when the time he had served was taken into account, his sentence was far less than the one Collins was now contemplating.

The judge got up to leave and the Court rose with him, emptying quickly now the end was known. The press poured into the Round Hall to separate and chase the various different reactions. Supt Scanlan led the posse first to the front gates of the Four Courts. He thanked his men and those that had helped from the US and Spain. He asked the press to respect the privacy of those who would have to come to terms with the fall out of the plot. Thankfully no one had lost their lives but it had been hard on all.

Then eventually it was Collins's solicitor again. Eugene O'Kelly spoke to the press as he had done after the verdict but this time he was alone. He said that Collins was grateful to P.J. Howard for his support.

'Ms Collins has been convicted by the jury and sentenced but most importantly she has been acquitted by her partner Mr Howard. She takes great comfort in the support that Mr Howard is showing and she has asked that I would apologise on her behalf for the great hurt and embarrassment and distress that has been caused to him by the use by the State of an incomplete letter which was taken out of context,' he said.

Once again the Gerry Ryan email got a mention. And once again Collins tried to minimise its damaging thrust but even at this late stage she stopped short of saying she had made the whole thing up.

'In addition Ms Collins is greatly upset by the intrusion of some elements of the press and I would ask on her behalf that there would be some dignity afforded to her. She has been subjected by an illegally held camera phone in the prison. Photographs have been taken of her in, what is in effect and will be for some time, her private residence. That is reprehensible and unacceptable.'

Then in a move that provided the tantalising glimpse of a curtain call, O'Kelly announced that Collins would indeed be fighting her conviction. There would indeed be an appeal so there was no point discussing the severity or not of the sentence. His statement finished, O'Kelly returned to the Four Courts and the media scrum disbanded to write up the story that would be on the front page of every paper the following day.

EPILOGUE

Despite all the revelations and allegations that had been presented to the court during her trial, despite every piece of evidence produced in proof of her many, profound betrayals, P.J. Howard said he was standing by Sharon Collins. For him she was no femme fatale, no scheming 'devil in the red dress'. She was simply the woman he loved, his companion of nine years, his nurse and his helper. His friend.

For Collins, sitting in her cell in the women's prison, there is probably considerable comfort to be taken from the knowledge that the man she had looked up to for most of her life, who had been her landlord and knight in shining armour, did not give up on her. The watching press and public might have shaken their heads in utter disbelief at his public display of trust after so profound a betrayal but for Collins there was still hope of a happy ever after.

The woman with the 'passive, detached but dependent' personality, who had plotted three murders would now pay the price for her involvement in the murderous conspiracy. But nothing had shaken P.J. Howard's steadfast belief in her. As Collins's solicitor had said, even if the jury had found her guilty, P.J. Howard himself had acquitted her.

In an interview with the *Sunday Times,* days after his appearance at the sentence hearing, Howard was emphatic in his belief that Collins was innocent.

'It's a waste of a good human being to put the likes of Sharon into jail. I don't think I'll be alive by the time Sharon serves her full term. I'm past my sell-by-date already. I want to set things right before I go,' he said.

In his strongest protestation of his love for Collins he told the paper, 'I wouldn't live in Ireland with Sharon but, if she'd have me, we would live somewhere away from everybody.' He couldn't have been more honest in revealing his true feelings.

For her co-accused, the self styled hitman who had failed so miserably at a life of crime, the outlook isn't quite so bright. He has no friends in Ireland. His wives have deserted him, his home was taken and the dazzling gaming tables of Vegas are now closed to him forever. Eid might be looking at a nearer release day but there will be no happy ever after for him.

When he finishes his sentence, it is likely that the FBI will want to speak to him about the Royston case. His future looks uncertain.

And so for 'the devil in the red dress' there is a silver lining of sorts. For all her scheming and plotting the chances are that she will be released before Christmas in 2012. The man she wanted to have killed has vowed to be there when she gets out. In other words there is still a chance of a happy ending somewhere far away from all the wreckage she has caused. In the meantime she will have time to read plenty of the blockbuster thrillers she so enjoyed and wonder at how her own life had come to mirror their twisting, turning plots.